Alleviating Global Poverty:
Technology for Economic and Social Uplift

**A Report of The Aspen Institute
International Peace, Security &
Prosperity Program**

**Nancy Bearg Dyke
Director, International Peace, Security
& Prosperity Program**
Editor

**Report of the Aspen Institute Conference
August 18–20, 2000
Aspen, Colorado**

PREVIOUS PUBLICATIONS OF THE INTERNATIONAL PEACE, SECURITY & PROSPERITY PROGRAM:

The International Poverty Gap: Investing in People and Technology to Build Sustainable Pathways Out

Persistent Poverty in Developing Countries: Determining the Causes and Closing the Gaps

Conflict Prevention: Strategies to Sustain Peace in the Post-Cold War World

Managing Conflict in the Post-Cold War World: The Role of Intervention

International Peace and Security in a New World System

To purchase copies of Aspen Institute publications please contact:

For all other inquiries, please contact:

The Aspen Institute
Publications Office
Phone: (410) 820-5326
Fax: (410) 827 9174
www.aspeninstitute.org/publications
E-mail: publications@aspeninstitute.org

The Aspen Institute
International Peace, Security &
Prosperity Program
Phone: (202) 736-5800
Fax: (202) 467-0790
www.aspeninstitute.org/ipsp

The conference summary and report reflect the sense of the group. The statements, conclusions, and recommendations therein should not be taken as the views of any particular participant or participant's employer unless noted otherwise.

Table of Contents

Foreword v

Preface by José María Figueres, Conference Chairman vii

Executive Summary 1

Report of Conference Dialogue and Recommendations

Introduction 15

The Role of Technology in a Development Strategy 19
    What Technology Cannot Do 19
    What Technology Can Do 20
    Building the Strategy 26

Choosing and Integrating Appropriate Technology 29
    Lessons Learned 29
    Complexity and Controversy in Choosing Appropriate Technology . . .31
    Scaling Up What Works 33
    Fundamental Constraints on Scaling Up Technology 34

Increasing Technology Access, Jobs and Resources 35
    Building Connectivity 35
    Scaling Up Tech-Related Businesses and Creating Jobs 37
    Broadening Access to Lower-Technology Products 39
    The Role of Government and Citizens in Developing Countries 41
    The Role of the International Community 43
    The Private Sector Role 44

Creating Virtuous Circles: The Human Element .49
    Leadership, Governance, and Empowerment 49
    Education, Migration, and a New Look at the Brain Drain 52
    Culture and Technological Change 56

Summary and Recommendations 59
    Principles for a Successful Technology-Infused Development Strategy .59
    General Recommendations for Players 62
    Some Specific Initiatives 66

Endnotes 69

Internet Links 72

Speeches

    Poverty and Technology: Meeting the Challenge
      Shashi Tharoor 75

Effective Poverty Reduction: Sustainable Development
and Information Technology
José María Figueres 79
Technology and Poverty
Bill Joy 87

Discussion Papers and Prepared Remarks

Loud and Near
Iqbal Quadir 91
Empowering the Poor: The Role of Technology
Edith Ssempala 113
Scaling Up Microfinance and Poverty Reduction
Jacques Attali 115
Poverty Alleviation and Renewable Energy in a Sustainable Context
Helena Chum 119
Broadband Via Satellite Reaches Everywhere
Santiago Ontañón 139

List of Conference Participants 145
Conference Agenda 147
Selected Readings and Internet Links 149
The Aspen Institute International Peace, Security & Prosperity Program . .157

Foreword

The value of an Aspen Institute conference or seminar is always the diversity of people around the table. This value is especially evident in the International Peace, Security & Prosperity global poverty conferences, which bring individuals from around the globe to share experiences and viewpoints in search of the best strategies and ideas for poverty alleviation, based on lessons learned from the past, recent trends, and new developments projected into the future. Through this search, they further the ideals of the Institute to promote enlightened, morally responsible leadership that addresses the new and continuing challenges in the 21st century.

The "Alleviating Global Poverty: Technology for Economic and Social Uplift" conference convened 22 diverse experienced and emerging leaders and experts from around the world in Aspen, Colorado, for roundtable dialogue on the role of technology in the alleviation of economic, political, social, and environmental poverty. The essence of their discussions, along with speeches and commissioned papers, is presented in this book. It is intended to be a useful, practical guide to how a range of technology can be harnessed to reduce the debilitating and limiting effects of poverty and provide opportunities to individuals and societies for their own advancement.

We would like to thank all who participated in the conference and added so much value to the dialogue and outcome, with special mention of those who made formal remarks or prepared papers. In particular, we thank the distinguished conference chairman, José María Figueres; the outstanding veteran conference moderator, Shashi Tharoor; and our esteemed trustee, His Royal Highness Prince Bandar bin Sultan. Prince Bandar has continued to support and demonstrate a high level of commitment to the International Peace, Security & Prosperity Program global poverty and conflict conferences, which have provided an invaluable forum for international dialogue and new thinking. His contributions are very much appreciated.

In addition, we want to acknowledge the excellent skills of Kevin Morrison as rapporteur, Marilyn Crane as conference planning assistant, and Stephanie Wethington as assistant editor of this book.

Elmer Johnson
President and CEO
The Aspen Institute

Nancy Bearg Dyke (Editor)
Director, International Peace,
   Security & Prosperity Program
The Aspen Institute

Preface by José María Figueres

Conference Chairman

We cannot escape the fact that global poverty remains a key challenge to peace and prosperity in the new century. The extent and consequences of poverty impact heavily and pose dangers to both the developing and developed parts of the world. For three days in August 2000, I was pleased to follow in the footsteps of Nelson Mandela and Jimmy Carter by serving as chairman of an Aspen Institute conference on alleviating global poverty. The conference *"Alleviating Global Poverty: Technology for Economic and Social Uplift"* was a round-table dialogue among an extraordinary international group of 25 individuals committed to exploring the role that technology can play in development and in closing the gap between the world's poor and rich.

Practicality, wisdom, creativity, and attention to lessons learned were all part of the discussion and are embodied in the strategy designed by the group and detailed in this report. A major conclusion of the conference was that technology adds significant value when applied to each element of a development strategy encompassing economic, social, political, and environmental efforts. This conclusion is also a fact that I have witnessed in my own country of Costa Rica in its strategy to overcome poverty and join the world economy.

A comprehensive development strategy enhanced by technology can work when the government and people take responsibility for their own development. They may accept a hand up from others in the form of technical assistance, new technology, and new ways to access technology or seed money to launch an endeavor. But, they don't expect a handout, and in fact, they would rather do the work themselves within their own cultural context.

My colleagues and I concluded that the value added by technology can make a substantial difference in eliminating poverty in the next 50 years if steps are taken to make it so. It is therefore crucial that poverty alleviation receive real action by the world community. In particular, the world community must utilize technology to even the playing field, so that the developing world can then spur its own progress forward towards a shared world in 2050 that is virtually free of devastating poverty.

I want to sincerely thank The Aspen Institute for holding this valuable conference and producing this useful book on the opportunities now at hand for concerted, productive action to end poverty.

Executive Summary

THE VISION

The picture on the cover of this book is a young girl with the familiar face of beauty, poverty, longing, and humanity. She represents one-half of the world's population—the three billion who live in wrenching poverty, and whose numbers could increase dramatically in the next 25 years with population growth in developing countries. Poor people are severely disadvantaged politically, economically, socially, and environmentally; they are largely left out of the political process and left behind in the rush of globalization and technological advance. The poor are also left behind on the international action agenda, as the problems of poverty receive more lip service than action.

This young girl is growing up in the early 21st century during a time of transforming technological change, knowledge, and added wealth—mostly in richer parts of the world. This Technology Revolution includes information technology, biotechnology, drugs to treat deadly disease like HIV/AIDS, solar power, other renewable energy resources, and other research and innovations. The developing world, however, has received very limited benefit from these remarkable advances in science and technology, and access to established technology is woefully deficient. Poverty persists.

Yet if the benefits of new and older technologies could reach this young girl and the people she represents, the most basic causes and effects of their poverty could be overcome. The three billion impoverished people around the globe struggling to survive on $1 or $2 a day could build a different future because they could break out of the cycle of poverty.

They could have clean water, medicine to fight disease, effective education, clean-burning fuel and a healthy home environment, nutritious and plentiful food, and less degradation of their environment and natural resources. They would have access to the Internet and other modern means of communicating, learning, receiving information, and doing business. After a solid basic education, this young girl and others could have the opportunity to construct their futures in their own countries, retaining their cultural identities while becoming productive members of the interconnected and interdependent world of the 21st century.

They also could gain more economic and political voice and eventually better governance, because information technology can empower people who are outside the channels of politics by giving them knowledge and voice to promote change. Increased transparency can yield governments that are more accountable, thus speeding steps toward creating the enabling environment that is necessary to attract foreign investment.

By 2050—and increasingly in the intervening years—the formerly poverty-stricken areas and people across the world could have a decent standard of living and opportunities to thrive and be economically integrated. No longer would there be a huge poverty gap, digital divide, or deadly disease gap between the developed and developing world. Undoubtedly, the world would still have an agenda of challenging problems to solve (and the evolving nature and ethics of some technological advance heighten those possibilities); but the envisioned world would be more equitable and ultimately more peaceful.

Is this vision achievable? How can the tremendous power and produced wealth of technology be most effectively and sustainably harnessed to alleviate poverty?

This critically important challenge was the subject of the third Aspen Institute International Peace, Security & Prosperity Program (IPSP) global poverty conference, "*Alleviating Global Poverty: Technology for Economic and Social Uplift*," held August 18-20, 2000, in Aspen, Colorado. The 22 participants were exceptionally experienced and thoughtful leaders from international institutions and key sectors of developing and developed countries. The conference chairman was former President of Costa Rica José María Figueres; the moderator was Shashi Tharoor, Director of Communications and Special Projects for the United Nations Secretary General. Previous chairmen of the IPSP global poverty conferences have included former Presidents Jimmy Carter and Nelson Mandela.

WHAT IS TECHNOLOGY TO ALLEVIATE POVERTY?

Technology to alleviate poverty often is assumed to be information technology; and, indeed, information technology has enormous, still-evolving potential to alleviate poverty and speed development. It is crucial to poverty alleviation in the 21st century.

Information technology, however, is not enough to successfully eliminate poverty. Other new and established technologies are essential to address effectively some of the key causes and effects of poverty, such as disease, hunger, unsafe drinking water, insufficient resources for agriculture, and degraded environments. Debilitating and immobilizing factors such as these must be overcome, or it will be impossible for people to improve their lives and be productive beyond mere survival. There are numerous low-technology products that can enable advances in human welfare. Technology does not have to be high tech to make a difference. *Thus, the vision of an end to global poverty depends upon a broad range of technologies—information technology, other new technologies, and older proven technologies.*

Human and technical factors are important factors in integrating technology into the lives of the poor. Technology to alleviate poverty must be "appropriate" to the situation to be successful. It must work for the people who will use it, and they must take ownership, operate, and maintain the technology. *Importantly, the technology must be compatible with the local culture as an enhancing, rather than homogenizing factor.* New technology often is controversial, and its use is heavily influenced by cultural, religious, and personal beliefs. In some cases, appropriate technology solutions to afflictions of poor people either do not yet exist or are too expensive for them to purchase. In some cases, complexity and controversy are slowing decision making because of issues of intellectual property and patent rights, cost recoupment for research and production, the effect on future research, and ethics. Some of the most prominent issues related to poverty alleviation are availability of HIV/AIDS drugs, research on other deadly diseases, and appropriateness of agricultural biotechnology.

Technology and its effects are continuing to evolve—creating new benefits and new challenges. In development, information technology is lessening the importance of economic distance, allowing countries to "leapfrog" development stages, and affecting the dynamics of governance by empowering ordinary citizens economically and politically. In an interesting twist, participants suggested that technology is beginning to alter some of the negative economic effects of "brain drain," as expatriates who moved to developed countries for more opportunity are generating increased revenues, knowledge, and new companies for their home countries. On the down side, the slowing of the information technology boom may decrease private sector resources readily available for transferring technology to the poor. And, Bill Joy of Sun Microsystems flagged the dual nature of new technology when he addressed the future ability of nanotechnology and robotics to create enough material goods to eliminate poverty while also creating negative effects on human life, such as international terrorism and corrosion of local cultures.

KEY CONFERENCE CONCLUSIONS AND RECOMMENDATIONS

- *Global poverty cannot be defeated unless poor people and countries have access to certain technology tools, including information and medical technology as a minimum.*

- *Global poverty can be eliminated within the next 50 years if a broad range of technology—not only information technology—is used as a tool to spark and enhance a comprehensive development strategy that encompasses economic, social, political, and environmental elements.*
- *Most of the technology tools and resources necessary to carry out this vision are within reach if decisions and commitments are made in the developed and developing worlds.*
- *Technology is not a solution in itself. Elimination of global poverty and spreading of the benefits of technology tools will not happen automatically.* **It will require:**
  - *Dedicated, focused planning, resources, cooperation, and action* by governments, private sectors, and civil societies of developed and developing countries and regional and international institutions—*to infuse appropriate technology into every element of development.*
  - *Expenditure and redirection of some of the considerable resources being generated by the Technology Revolution toward development purposes;*
  - *"Scaling up" technology tools that work successfully to alleviate poverty—* from low technology to high technology—*to reach many millions more poor people;*
  - *Creating access for poor people to the right technology* so that they can use it, along with other tools and their own initiative, to pull themselves up from poverty.
  - *Resources, initiatives, and responsibility by developing country* governments and their people to help create the necessary conditions to reduce poverty, including good governance.
  - *Attention to human elements* such as governance, culture, and leadership, necessary for technology to achieve its maximum benefit; and
  - *Sustained leadership, commitment, and engagement.*

Elements of the Strategy

A technology-infused comprehensive development strategy as envisioned by the conference participants would have the following main features, which speak to both technical and human considerations:

- *Priority must be given to appropriate technology as a key component in every sector.* Appropriate technology fills a basic need, is usable and culturally accepted by the local population, and is sustainable.
- *Significantly more resources* from governments, institutions, and the private sector *must be dedicated and applied on a sustained basis for technology-related development, and on the basis of improved two-way communication between donors and recipients on development needs and priorities..*

- *More technological research must be done,* for example, in health, water, agriculture, and environment, to solve problems that primarily afflict the poor.

- *Foreign investment must be spread* to the poorest countries.

- *Good governance, including conquering corruption, must be a pillar* of the strategy, along with deregulation and other aspects of an investment-friendly environment.

- *Poor people and countries should have access to and take ownership of technology and be empowered and responsible* to construct and develop their own futures. This is true at all political and economic levels of society, including people in power and those without power (the "ins" and the "outs.")

- *Health and education must be pillars* of the strategy and should be the subject of a national strategic plan that incorporates technology in each developing country.

- *Vibrant higher education institutions and a strong research base are critical to development* and to avoiding "brain drain" by retaining educated citizens—or attracting them back.

- *Technology processes and products that are successful for the poor should be identified and scaled up*—replicated and made accessible to millions more people—throughout societies to reach everyone who could benefit.

- *Connectivity must be increased.*

- *Development and utilization of renewable energy sources and applications must be pursued for sustainable development and poverty alleviation.*

- *Resources must be made available for entrepreneurs to start up technology-related small and medium businesses* that create jobs and build middle classes, as well as to enlarge the availability of microcredit funds for microentrepreneurs.

- *Culture must be recognized and respected* for its role in a society's acceptance or non-acceptance of new technology.

- *Leaders throughout the world must monitor technological developments* closely for potential new tools or negative effects in the fight against poverty, *then act on the information* in a *timely* and pro-development manner.

General Recommendations for Players – Roles and Resources

Enacting the strategy requires action, cooperation, and leadership by the major public and private sector and civil society players in development. The following "action lists" suggest the most important roles and tasks they could undertake separately and in collaboration to give life to a comprehensive technology-infused development strategy.

♠ *Governments and Multilateral Institutions—Action List*

Governments of developing and developed countries will be key in facilitating the use of technology for poverty reduction, beginning with providing for basic needs to be met. Developing country governments have responsibility for their people and for conditions in their countries. Only they can provide the regulatory environment and proper incentives for the private sector to act most efficiently in incorporating technology that developed country governments, multilateral institutions, and corporations can help make available. Developed countries and multilateral institutions can assist in funding the policy, regulatory reforms, and institution building required to ensure widespread access to technology.

♠ *Developing Countries*

- *Adopt* a two-part strategy that includes technologies that can improve human conditions and promote growth.
- *Give* high priority in allocating financial resources to developing human resources—especially health care and universal primary and secondary education. Also, fund technology-driven change that can speed up development and entry into the world economy.
- *Institute* sound economic policies and an environment of good governance and rule of law that encourages openness, innovation, and private sector competition and attracts foreign investment. Stop corruption.
- *Carry* out steps to integrate technology and make it accessible to citizens. Streamline regulations and bureaucratic requirements.
- *Build* higher education into a national development asset that advances the country, provides an important research base, retains the best and brightest citizens, and attracts expatriates to return.
- *Offer* incentives and seed money to entrepreneurs and businesses of all sizes; consider creating technology centers, such as the one in Bangalore, India.
- *Fund* replications of programs that have worked.
- *Manage* the electromagnetic spectrum and other technology-related public goods to the best development benefit for the country. For example, some countries sell or rent some bandwidth; these proceeds should benefit the whole country.
- *Facilitate* involvement by overseas nationals, utilize their skills, and draw on their resources to promote national development and mitigate the negative impact of the brain drain.

- *Create* national networks in education, health care, technology information infrastructure, and other sectors to coordinate resources and services available to combat poverty.

♠ *Developed Countries and Multilateral Institutions*

- *Focus* high priority on how best to assist national governments in their fight against poverty, including how specific technologies can be used most effectively in that fight. *The most effective way to provide external assistance is to facilitate placing ownership and responsibility in the hands of the people themselves.*

- *Communicate* with the leaders and ordinary people of poor countries and listen to their expressed needs.

- *Boost* international aid flows (which have been in decline over the past decade), with particular emphasis on increasing usable funding channeled to technology-related development programs, policy reform, and institutional development.

- *Learn* from programs that have worked, and fund multiple similar programs.

- *Partner* with the private sector, including business, NGOs, foundations, and universities.

- *Create* new incentives, subsidies, and funding for government and businesses of all sizes in developing countries to access development-related technology.

- *Arrange* programs in which developing countries are models for other developing countries, and facilitate experience-sharing generally.

♠ *Corporate Private Sector—Action List*

The corporate private sector benefits from advances in new technologies, and enormous amounts of new wealth will be created over the next 50 years. A sense of morality asserts that wealth should be spread, but so does business sense: as more people participate in growth, there will be more consumers. Business training, philanthropy, and reinvestment by corporations in local communities can enhance the business environment, human capital, and overall productivity of the area, to the benefit of the local people and the corporation.

♠ *Corporate Private Sector of Developing Countries*

- *Seek out* opportunities to promote and help fund human resources programs that drive development, including health, training, and education services for the poor.

- *Pay* taxes.
- *Invest* in local communities; funnel some profits back to the community.
- *Build* supportive relationships with national higher education and training institutions; form partnerships with the colleges and universities of industrialized countries.
- *Fund* replications of projects that have worked.
- *Form* professional associations to strengthen civil society, utilizing communications technology.

♠ Corporate Private Sector of Developing Countries

- *Increase and distribute* investment flows more widely to poor countries as their investment climates improve.
- *Fund* research for problems that are common to poor populations, such as malnutrition and tropical diseases.
- *Subsidize* some technology transfer and the cost of new technology.
- *Seek* innovative solutions to the problems of poor people.
- *Support* local communities in poor countries through technology, such as providing computers to schools.
- *Engage* in partnerships with the higher education institutions of developing countries.

♠ Civil Society—Action List

Civil society at the national and international levels plays a fundamental role in governance and the adaptation of technology, and its role is being enhanced by new technologies.

♠ Civil Society of Developing Countries

(Citizens, grassroots groups, media, NGOs, religious institutions, philanthropists, universities, expatriates, interest groups, professional associations)

- *Take advantage* of and build on the benefits of technology (such as enhanced transparency of government and easier communication with others inside and outside the country) that can lead to improved governance and an empowered citizenry.
- *Demand* specific government actions that foster an enabling environment for foreign investment, technology, and entrepreneurship.
- *Create* networks that can influence government decision making to increase access by the society and its poor to technology.

◆ Private Non-corporate/Civil Society of Developed Countries

(NGOs, foundations, individual philanthropists, media, universities, religious institutions)

- **Seek out** opportunities to promote and help fund human resources programs and research that underpin or drive development, including health, training, basic education services, and universities.
- **Work with and directly fund** developing country civil society elements, especially by taking advantage of technology.
- **Create or join** networks than can affect economic and political decisions at the international level by linking interest groups within different countries and across borders. Conference participants thought this action would be particularly important in the context of women's health.
- **Fund** replications of successful projects that developing countries want to adopt.

◆ Some Specific Initiatives

Many tasks can be addressed effectively by more than one actor, and often initiatives depend on collaborative approaches across sectors. Several such initiatives were identified in the conference.

Increase Technology-Related Foreign Aid

Governments and multilateral institutions should provide more discretionary foreign assistance funding for technology-related projects in developing countries. It starts with incorporating a "technology mentality" into all development objectives (from agricultural development to improvements in health service delivery to microenterprise) and ensuring sufficient discretionary resources for these efforts. Such funding should be provided for:

- policy and regulatory reform required to ensure widespread access to and use of technology within countries;
- promising pilot programs across sectors to encourage innovation;
- replicating successful programs and projects;
- promoting digital opportunities, including exploration of cross-sectoral links to enhance education and access to education, and to address the educational needs of the countries hardest hit by HIV/AIDS;
- facilitating and funding projects between less-advanced developing countries and more-advanced developing countries to provide an appropriate model and beneficial practical advice.

Replicate Successful Technology Products and Processes

Corporations, private sponsors, foundations, governments, and institutions should make available to poor countries and people the products or processes that have proven successful in similar circumstances elsewhere. Several examples from this report are electronic community centers, capital and business training for small and medium-size businesses, manual water pumps, solar-powered water purifiers, biomass and charcoal clean-burning stoves—buy the stoves or "adopt a village" and enable it to set up stove production.

Emphasize Women's Health with Research and Technology

Governments and institutions, foundations and NGOs, civil society, researchers, and the private sector all have a role to play in promoting advances in women's health care and helping to make such advances available to all women. Women's health is inextricably tied to the development of a country, thus increasing women's access to good health facilities, practices, and products is crucial. Conference participants particularly noted the need for greater use of existing education methods, condoms and more research into alternative contraceptive methods to inhibit the spread of HIV/AIDS and other infectious diseases and reduce high birth rates.

Expand Distance Learning and Develop Language Availability

The private sector, in cooperation with national governments and institutions of higher learning, should continue to develop distance-learning programs with translations that can be used by people in poor and remote areas.

Establish Professional Associations in Developing Countries

Multilateral institutions, journalists, business people, NGOs, chambers of commerce, and governments can invest in the development of professional associations in developing countries to foster national expertise and standards and to strengthen civil society and its voice in governance.

Develop National Talent Banks to Assist Development

Governments, businesses, universities, and professional associations should facilitate links between citizens abroad and at home, for example, an Internet "talent bank" of expatriates who can advise government and business on technology and development. This type of resource may ameliorate some of the effects of the "brain drain."

Establish University Links and Research

Governments, NGOs, and businesses should encourage links between universities in different countries in an effort to strengthen higher education and promote cross-country learning that enhances the development process and empowers the national elite. This strategy includes "south-south" cooperation between developing countries, as well as "triangular" cooperation among a rich country, a middle-income country, and a poor country.

Initiatives Identified for Further Exploration

Explore Technology Subsidies/Subsidy Fund - International institutions, the G-8, and corporations could explore further the types of subsidies or subsidy funds that could help developing countries and small and medium-size businesses pay the high price of technological advancements that could benefit them but are protected by property rights. Attention is being given to medicines, but the principle also applies to patented software.

Explore Template for Connectivity - Public-sector institutions and NGOs could explore whether a "template" for connectivity in developing countries would be useful in providing countries with a guide about the deregulation and other steps necessary for countries to take in order for telecommunication industries to be most effective and efficient and provide connectivity to the whole society. Such a template could be a useful tool for business and civil society in encouraging their governments to take the required steps.

Explore a Small and Medium-Size Business Development Bank - The public and private sectors could explore the idea of a small and medium-size business development bank within an established institution or as a separate entity, capitalized by private-sector contributors and international institutions. Such a hybrid bank possibly could work through NGOs and the private sector as intermediaries, and it could provide business–related technical assistance as well as funding.

Further work should be done on several areas of extreme importance for poverty reduction, including biotechnology, global warming/climate change, and how to deal with the long-term effects of AIDS devastation on societies and economies.

CONCLUSION

Much like the Industrial Revolution, the Technology Revolution is an ongoing process with several strands, not a single or easily definable event. It is evolving, as are its products and effects. The full story will be told later in the century after more exploration and innovation, success and failure, risk taking and status quo, lessons learned and lessons ignored.

We do know in this first year of the 21st century that technology tools undoubtedly can ameliorate much of the suffering and poverty in the developing world. Deliberate actions are needed to enable the world's poor to thrive in their own social and cultural contexts and expand the depth and breadth of their participation in the world community. Infusing appropriate technology into development through resources, action, and cooperative effort by governments, the private sector, and the civil societies of developed and developing countries can remove the scourge of poverty from the world in the next 50 years. Participants in the "*Alleviating Global Poverty: Technology for Economic and Social Uplift*" conference called on leaders everywhere to supply the critical elements that can make it happen: political will and visionary leadership.

Report of Conference

Dialogue and Recommendations

Report of Conference Dialogue and Recommendations

"The impact of globalization and technology gives us an opportunity to reach out and to engage poor people in a way such that they can construct and develop their own futures."[a]

INTRODUCTION

The Aspen Institute poverty conference *"Alleviating Global Poverty: Technology for Economic and Social Uplift"* convened in August 2000 at a time when inequality and wrenching poverty still inhibit the individual and collective advancement of one-half of the world's people. Statistics describing global poverty and its negative effects, such as disease, illiteracy, malnourishment, and unemployment, abound.

Poor people are severely disadvantaged politically, economically, and socially; they are largely left out of the political process and left behind in the gold rush of globalization and new technology. To quote conference chairman José María Figueres, "There is no trickle down." The poor also are left behind on the international action agenda, as the problems of poverty receive more lip service than action.

Despite the affliction of poverty on so much of humanity early in the 21st century, the participants in the conference shared a vision of 50 years into the future—a world free of poverty and its debilitating and limiting effects.

How do we get from here to there, when poverty has proven to be a deeply entrenched foe even in the midst of unparalleled economic prosperity? In the past three decades, more than 20 industrialized states and more than a dozen developing countries have succeeded in eliminating extreme poverty, yet human impoverishment remains devastatingly widespread. The vast majority of the poor have not had access to new research and technologies related to information, health, agriculture, biology, and energy, all of which can change lives fundamentally. The poverty gap between the "haves" and the "have nots" persists. With it come inequality, conflict, and misery around the world; these ills negatively affect poor people disproportionately, but they affect the rich as well.

The persistence of poverty—and the frustration it breeds in those who try to fight it—often lead either to resignation or to a tendency to look for "quick fixes" and "silver bullets." In today's world, many are touting technology as the missing link that can allow poor countries to catch up with their rich counterparts. Indeed, the Technology Revolution that began late in the 20th century already has produced wealth, opportunity, and breathtaking change. Estimates of the wealth that new and emerging technologies could generate over the next 50 years soar into the trillions of US dollars. Thus far, however, the benefits of the Technology Revolution have been spread markedly unevenly. For a variety of reasons, poor people and poor countries around the world simply do not have adequate access to technology that can benefit them. They lack the resources, infrastructure, and often the quality of governance and the business environment that attracts the foreign investment necessary to bring technology to their countries. The international community lacks an integrated strategy and commitment of resources.

Nevertheless, *technology holds enormous promise for the world's poor to finally overcome poverty and its ill effects.* Some of the possibilities have been put to work successfully in the developing world, for example in medicine, education, renewable energy applications, and communication. Experience has

One challenge is to determine how best to identify technologies of all types that can change the lives of the poor.

been accumulating regarding what works and what does not work. Technologies and the means of creating access to them are still evolving, which creates even more possibilities for the future. Many hopes for progress against poverty in the developing world are riding on technology, especially information and communication technology (ICT), as demonstrated by work of the Group of 8 (G-8) industrialized countries, G-15 developing countries, and others.[1] *The challenge is to determine how best to identify technologies **of all types** that can change the lives of the poor, remain abreast of new developments, and scale up the successes to reach broadly and deeply throughout the developing world to empower people to chart their own futures and end their poverty.*

The *Alleviating Global Poverty: Technology for Economic and Social Uplift* conference was convened August 18-20, 2000, in Aspen, Colorado, to review the current and future potential of technology to speed development and to suggest a broad strategy for harnessing technology to help lift the world's poor out of poverty. It was the third conference in the global poverty series of the Aspen Institute International Peace, Security & Prosperity Program, which has brought together leaders of diverse experiences and perspectives from around the world for in-depth roundtable dialogue to seek out the most effective strategies and best practices for alleviating poverty. The conferences have included an ongoing and deepening discussion of technology in the context of globalization and development.

The August 2000 conference was attended by 22 outstanding public- and private- sector leaders in development and technology, leading journalists and academics, and other high-level representatives of developed and developing countries. The conference chairman was José María Figueres, former President of Costa Rica. The moderator was Shashi Tharoor, Director of Communications and Special Projects for the UN Secretary General. Conference dialogue was centered around key questions such as: Can information technology and other new and emerging technologies close the gap between rich and poor? What role do technologies play now—and what role can they play in the future—in development? How can the tremendous power and produced wealth of technology be most effectively and sustainably harnessed for the poor? What role do governments, the private sector, international institutions, and others play? Where are the resources to be found? What is the role of culture? Of leadership?

The major conclusions of the conference were that: *Poverty can be eliminated within the next 50 years if a broad range of technology—not only information technology—is used as a tool to spark and enhance a comprehensive development strategy that encompasses economic, political, social, and environmental elements. Technology is not a solution in itself, but it has enormous potential to speed poverty reduction. Elimination of global poverty and spreading of the benefits of technology will not happen automatically. It will require careful planning—by regional and international institutions and governments of developed and developing countries, along with their private sectors and civil societies—to take full advantage of technology developments from low to high technology. It also will require significant resources produced by the Technology Revolution to solve root problems that cause poverty to persist. Developing countries and their people must be responsible for constructing their own futures; however, planning, leadership, and commitment from governments, private sectors, and civil society throughout the developed and developing worlds must make it happen.*

Poverty can be eliminated within the next 50 years if a broad range of technology—not only information technology—is used as a tool to spark and enhance a comprehensive development strategy that encompasses economic, political, social, and environmental elements.

This report outlines the key considerations and building blocks for a global poverty alleviation strategy driven by technology as envisioned by the conference participants. It includes lessons learned about what has been proven to work and how to scale up those practices and products, as well as how to encourage new ideas and initiatives. The reader is provided with a set of principles, technical and human elements considered essential to successful use of technology in development, and key roles and tasks. It includes several specific recommendations and technology project examples to be enacted or further explored by leaders and policy makers in government and civil society, corporate sponsors, and entrepreneurs who want to take effective action to reduce poverty—to make a real difference.

The report is based around three days of conference discussions and is not an exhaustive study of what technology can do. Its primary value is in the principles and general recommendations—supported by good examples—reached by informed dialogue of wise, experienced, and forward-thinking representatives from relevant sectors of the developed and developing worlds.

THE ROLE OF TECHNOLOGY IN A DEVELOPMENT STRATEGY

In considering the role of technology in a development strategy, participants felt it was important to establish what technology tools can and cannot do, including how it is challenging conventional wisdom about the dynamics of development and poverty.

Importantly, technology was defined along a broad spectrum that includes more than information and communications. In its broadest definition, technology to alleviate poverty is "any innovative technique that represents an advance on current ways of doing things, that saves time and labor, that enhances productivity, and that improves the lives of the very poor." The definition therefore encompasses many technologies, from less advanced to highly advanced.

What Technology Cannot Do

Technology is not a panacea, or a silver bullet, or an end in itself. It would be wishful thinking to assume that technology on its own momentum and power will eradicate poverty. Technology by itself cannot eradicate poverty. Technology cannot replace the need for strong leadership and human interactions. Without effort, additional resources, and long-term commitment by people who can increase access to technology and those who may benefit from it, technology by itself cannot fulfill its potential in development. It is true that repressive and corrupt governments too often control and limit access for many people to the potential benefits of technology, but it also is obvious that *technology alone cannot reach everyone—especially the poorest of the poor—without deliberate effort.*

There is a parallel with the 1997 Aspen Institute poverty conference, at which participants concluded that free markets and globalization alone are not enough to overcome poverty. They recommended a "Market Plus" strategy to supplement the market and ensure broad-based growth and the well being of the poor, particularly in the earliest stages of development.[2] Similarly, at the 2000 conference, participants cited the need for "Technology Plus."

Technology's limited role is evident in education, a key factor in development. Participants at the conference related many stories of the ability of poor people—particularly young people—to learn quickly how to use computers and the Internet. Such skills, however, will be only marginally helpful without functional literacy. The UN estimates that the adult illiteracy rate in the least developed countries is about 50%. The youth illiteracy rate in the same countries is about 38%.[3] Although software that will enable voice transcription is being developed, it is likely to elude the poorest people for a long time, especially if they do not speak a major language. Strong education policies, including literacy programs, in developing countries remain essential if development is to occur—and if technology is to contribute to that development as knowledge becomes increasingly important in the world economy.

Another example relates to the potential of online markets. Although the Internet may be an effective way of marketing and distributing goods and services, most small-scale individual producers in developing countries (such as coffee farmers) cannot use the Internet to market their products directly, bypassing middlemen. Even setting aside issues of connectivity, small-scale farmers have to be organized to accumulate an exportable quantity, reduce transaction costs, gain access to processing services typically required for exporting, ensure quality control, and deal with government and market requirements for exportation.[4]

These examples illustrate how the ability to use technology can be limited by lack of skills or organization. Other limitations can be related simply to access or behavior. For example, the existence of HIV/AIDS drugs does not mean they are available to all who need them. Most drugs are still not available to millions of people because of cost and patent issues. As for behavior, technology can produce safe drinking water, but people need to be trained in hand washing and other behavior so that the benefits of the clean water are not inadvertently countered. Low levels of education and literacy make such training harder. Technology, then, can be of limited use in fighting poverty unless it is placed in an environment of supportive policies and initiatives. As the following section explains, however, if those supportive policies exist, technology can put a charge into the development process. (Information technology can be an exception because it can circumvent bad government policies, as described in a later chapter.)

The existence of technology by itself does not ensure effective access to it by those who need it.

What Technology Can Do

Technology can make a positive difference in all major sectors of society—social, economic, political, and environmental. Thus, technology can be a strengthening and reinforcing component in the kind of comprehensive development approach that is being touted by the World Bank, the United Nations Development Programme (UNDP), and others in the development community.[5]

Transforming Lives Through Economic, Social, and Political Uplift

Technological change can enable citizens and governments to alter dynamics on two levels to break out of cycles that perpetuate poverty. *First,* technology can improve survival rates and quality of life by directly addressing basic needs, such as disease prevention, clean water, health care, basic education, and energy. *Second,* information, communications, and other advanced technologies are tools that can enable poor individuals and countries to establish their own economic, social, and political uplift more rapidly than before. In the early 21st century, information is empowering and enabling; and technology is a strong and evolving tool to acquire information in all sectors.

Used in the right away, technology has the potential to dramatically alter human lives by improving economic prospects, eliminating debilitating and deadly diseases, enabling educational and cultural opportunities, or stimulating better governance. Already, technology tools have demonstrated a role in facilitating the basics of health, education, energy, and communication to significant numbers of poor people in efforts to overcome some of the worst problems of poverty. Some examples follow:

Technology has the potential to dramatically alter human lives by improving economic prospects, eliminating debilitating and deadly diseases, enabling educational and cultural opportunities, or stimulating better governance.

In areas of *health, agriculture, energy and environment,* the application of technology includes :

- Water purification;
- Vaccines to prevent disease and medications to slow the course of disease or cure it;
- Cloth to filter water to prevent guinea worm;
- Further research into new vaccines, including those that do not require refrigeration;
- Condoms to prevent the spread of sexually transmitted diseases and unplanned pregnancies;
- Mosquito netting to aid in the prevention of malaria;
- Internet or videos for basic health training and information;
- Internet to enable physicians to communicate with other physicians and transmit lab records;
- Renewable sources of energy for electricfication and fuel;
- Genetically modified foods that are heartier and healthier;
- Agricultural reform through biomass technologies that improve production of food and feed; and
- Cleaner-burning fuel and alternatives to using non-renewable resources as fuel.

In *education,* the application of technology can support:

- Basic, higher, and continuing education augmented by resources available on the Internet;
- Distance learning, up-to-date teaching materials, libraries, encyclopedias, and means of communicating with other researchers in other parts of the world through the Internet; and

- Cooperative programs with other schools, universities, and communities.

In *communication*, the application of technology can provide:

- Support to organize and operate policy and grassroots networks that promote the interests or needs of underrepresented people;
- The spread of information about markets and the opportunity to sell products to a wider audience at competitive prices;
- More rapid and timely communication and availability of vastly more information in every sector;
- Cellular telephony and satellites for communication in rural areas that have little or no telephone infrastructure;
- Increased transparency of government and more open societies; and
- Access to formerly unreachable markets.

Overall, the application of technology tools can promote:

- The breaking of cycles of disease, bad governance, corruption, isolation, lack of education, and economic distress;
- Job creation, business development, an enhanced research base, productivity, and economic growth;
- Empowerment of the disadvantaged so that they gain a political voice;
- Anti-corruption efforts through increased transparency;
- Decreased environmental degradation;
- Faster development; and
- Sustainable development.

Box 1 lists some of the stories and examples from the conference that illustrate the power of technology to bring about change in the lives of poor individuals. Boxes 3 through 7 feature additional examples.

Box 1 — Examples of the Transforming Power of Technology: Successful Models

E-commerce — In Ethiopia, an entrepreneur farmer sets up a website to sell sheep and goats, aimed at the expatriate community in Canada and the United States. Family members and friends in those countries can now buy the goats for their family members back home using credit cards or other forms of payment.

Microcredit and cell phones — In Bangladesh, a woman using a microcredit loan buys a cellular phone and then sells the inexpensive phone service to neighbors. She not only provides the service of connectivity to her village community, she also makes a living for herself and her family. Her whole neighborhood has the potential of new economic opportunities. But look out for competition: a young woman in the village has just bought a computer and will soon be selling Internet services...

box continued on next page

Electronic community centers — In Costa Rica, a small foundation promotes rudimentary technology centers that allow villagers to access the Internet, for personal communication, telehealth, e-commerce, and computer education services. Using one of the centers to communicate directly with buyers, a coffee grower triples the price at which he can sell his coffee. Using the Internet, a poor community learns how to grow aquatic horticulture from a Web page—and does so.[1]

HIV/AIDS prevention — Since 1995, Thailand has conducted HIV testing and counseling for pregnant women, and provided replacement formula and regimens of AZT. These actions have dramatically reduced the number of infants who contract HIV from their mothers during birth and through breast milk. These cost-effective preventative measures result in healthier babies and lower HIV/AIDS prevalence, and they brighten prospects for social and economic growth as children are able to attend school and parents are healthier and able to care for them.[2]

Water purification — In a Palestinian village near Hebron, a solar-powered ultraviolet water purifier with the potential to provide 7.9 million liters of water annually—enough for approximately 2200 people—has been installed as part of an electronic community center. As a result, the incidence of water-borne disease and related deaths has decreased, improving the population's life span and quality of life. (In the developing world as a whole, 400 children die every hour from water-borne disease.) [3]

River blindness — In Africa, young children lead blind parents, aunts, uncles, and grandparents from place to place. River blindness (onchocerciasis) affects an estimated 18 million people, causing debilitating itching and vision loss. The blindness prevents individuals from working, and the fear of the disease chases people from fertile riverbanks. With the distribution of Mectizan, a preventative drug, the incidence of the disease has dropped and people are returning to some of the fertile riverbank villages to farm.[4]

1. See http://www.entebbe.com (in spanish), http://www.lincos.net, and http://media.mit.edu

2. World Bank, "Thailand's Response to AIDS: Building on Success, Confronting the Future." 2000, p.30. Available at:
http://www.worldbank.org.th/social/pdf/Thailand's%20Response%20to%20AIDS.pdf

3. Greenstar, see http://www.greenstar.org/pressroom/TIME%20Telecenters.htm and http://ww.greenstar.org/components.htm.

4. The Carter Center, "River Blindness." See http://www.cartercenter.org/riverblindness.html.

of development as *technology allows more rapid or enhanced development and plays a role in promoting more open governance and grassroots empowerment.* In par-

Technology allows more rapid or enhanced development and plays a role in promoting more open governance and grassroots empow-erment.

ticular, information technology is lessening the impor-tance of "economic distance," calling into doubt the "staged" approach to development, and affecting the dynamics of governance and views of the brain drain. In addition, technologies and their effects are still evolving, which can further affect the dynamics of development. (See Bill Joy's conference remarks in this volume on posi-tive and negative potential.)

Distance Matters Less

In the past, one of the common assumptions about development has been that "economic distance matters," that is, that the geographic, trade, regulatory, or time barriers between people and countries affect economic relationships. Technology is altering this situation to some degree, particu-larly with regard to geographic distance. Especially with cheaper and more instantaneous and constant communications, the geographic distance sep-arating people, cities, companies, or governments matters less and does not constrain the potential for trade and communication as significantly as in the past. Products can be manufactured or services rendered a continent away from the home office or customer, with operations ongoing 24 hours a day. The Internet can be used to transmit intellectual work, as well as fac-tual information, sales, and accounting at the touch of a button. The field of electronic-commerce (e-commerce)—which is at a fledgling stage in the developing world—is one manifestation of the potential of trade through the Internet. For example, an Internet website called the Virtual Souk pro-vides direct access to international markets for several hundred artisans from the Middle East (many of them women). Participating artisans receive 65-80% of the proceeds more than what they receive when they deal through traditional channels.[6] In addition, satellites are providing a means to bridge distance and time over infrastructure gaps.

Stages of Development: Straight-Line or Leapfrog?

A long-standing view holds that countries must move gradually through conventional "stages" of development. *Technology can enable them to skip stages, especially if they emphasize human capital and areas in which the impact of the infor-mation revolution will have a particularly high relative payoff.* Some observers have termed this process "leapfrogging"—essentially, skipping phases of development (such as going from no telephone lines at all in rural areas to cell phones, skipping the expensive step of building land-line infrastruc-ture).

While such leapfrogging yields clear economic benefits for some citizens, it can leave others behind, and resources that would have gone toward their basic human needs and infrastructure development are diverted. Leapfrog advocates argue that moving ahead with technology can spur, speed, and spread economic and social progress faster than a straight-line progression through the stages. Some straight-line advocates would argue that new technological advances benefit the elites at the expense of common people and that national resources must be used first to meet basic needs before new technology is infused to promote rapid development. There is not clear consensus on the value of leapfrogging or its feasibility in broad economic terms. Although leapfrogging has great potential in certain circumstances (typically at the sector level), critics assert that if the basics of water, sanitation, nutrition, and education are not available, information and communications technology will be an impractical and unusable tool for the poor.

As societies resist change, issues of culture also play heavily in the leapfrogging versus straight-line debate, as described in the section on "Culture and Technological Change."

Governance: Dynamics of Change

Good governance—open, accountable, and responsive to the people—has long been considered critical to development, including as a basis for attracting private capital investment and new technology. *Where good governance does not exist, technology has the potential to act as a policy-changing instrument. Technology can have a dynamic role in stimulating good governance because it can partially circumvent bad government and ultimately change the quality of government by empowering people from below with more information and economic power.*

The interrelationship between technology and governance is discussed in greater detail later in this report and in Iqbal Quadir's conference paper.

> **Where good governance does not exist, technology has the potential to act as a policy-changing instrument. It can partially circumvent bad government and ultimately change the quality of government by empowering people from below with more information and economic power.**

Brain Drain Dynamics May Have a Silver Lining

The conventional wisdom about the severe negative impacts of the "brain drain" is evolving in a very interesting way due to technology, as evidenced in conference discussions. Technology is beginning to alter some of the negative economic effects of brain drain as expatriates generate increasing technology-related revenues, knowledge, and new companies for their home countries. Depending on the stage at which one measures the value added, technology might make the problems of brain drain less severe, as discussed in more detail later in this report.

Building the Strategy

To sum up what technology can do, a quote from conference participant and co-founder of Sun Microsystems Bill Joy is in order: "In the 21st century, science and technology will give us the tools to achieve mastery over the physical world, to the limits of physical law...I am optimistic that the new technologies will soon create enough material goods that we can choose to eliminate poverty and give everyone basic health care" (and other basics). "But," he continued, voicing a view shared by other participants in the conference as well, "that alone is not sufficient—in a post-scarcity world we must also help people find meaning in their lives." (See Bill Joy's conference remarks in this volume.)

"I am optimistic that the new technologies will soon create enough material goods that we can choose to eliminate poverty." - Bill Joy

In light of the enormous potential of technology to speed reduction of global poverty and enhance the human condition, conference participants recommended a development strategy driven by technology to spur economic, social, political, and environmental development. Such a strategy would have the following main features, which speak to both the material and more human considerations:

- *It should be a comprehensive development strategy with high priority on appropriate technology as a key component in every sector.*

Practical, efficient technology solutions to problems of poverty and building productivity should be actively considered and incorporated into every element of a comprehensive development strategy.

- *Practical, efficient technology solutions* to problems of poverty and building productivity *should be actively considered and incorporated* into every element of a comprehensive development strategy.

- *Significantly more resources* from governments, institutions, and the private sector *must be dedicated and applied* on a sustained basis for technology-related development.

- *More technological research must be done* to solve problems that primarily afflict the poor.

- *Foreign investment must be spread* to the poorest countries.

- *Poor people and countries should be empowered and responsible* to construct and develop their own futures, which technology makes possible.

- *Good governance, including conquering corruption, must be a pillar* of the strategy, along with deregulation and other aspects of an investment-friendly environment.

- *Health and education must be pillars* of the strategy and should be the subject of a national strategic plan that incorporates technology in each country.

- *Higher education should be built into a national development asset* that advances the country, provides an important research base, retains the best and brightest citizens, and attracts expatriates to return.

- *Technology processes and products that are successful for the poor should be massively scaled up or replicated, diffused broadly, and made accessible* throughout societies to reach the grass roots and everyone who could benefit.
- *Connectivity must be increased.*
- *Development and utilization of renewable energy sources and applications must be pursued* for sustainable development and poverty alleviation.
- *Resources must be made available for entrepreneurs to start up technology-related small and medium businesses* that create jobs, as well as to enlarge the availability of microcredit funds for microentrepreneurs.
- *Culture must be recognized and respected* for its role in a society's acceptance of new technology.
- *Leaders throughout the world must monitor technological developments* closely for potential new tools or negative effects in the fight against poverty, *then act on the information* in a timely and pro-development manner.

These building blocks for successfully executing the strategy are covered in the next chapters.

CHOOSING AND INTEGRATING APPROPRIATE TECHNOLOGY

Experience shows that technology can play a key role in development, but it must be chosen and used appropriately. The *"appropriateness" of any technology for solving a specific problem in a poor community is determined not by whether the technology is high-tech or low-tech, off-the-shelf or newly developed, but simply by whether the technology works in a given situation* (see Box 2). What works for one country, region, or sector of society will not necessarily work for another. Different people and areas have diverse needs and capacities to adopt and absorb new technology, which then must be maintained after donors leave to be effective. In much of the developing world, technology must be operable and maintainable by people who are not educated and may have basic or no skills. In some cases, a local population must be trained and able to train others in use and repair of the technology.

> The "appropriateness" of any technology for solving a specific problem in a poor community is determined by whether the technology works in that situation.

Technology is not only the latest advances in biomedical science, computers, and satellites—it is a spectrum from low-tech to high-tech. As Bill Joy, Co-Founder and Chief Scientist of Sun Microsystems, pointed out at the October 1999 Aspen Institute poverty conference, "There are many off-the-shelf and near-in technologies that can be deployed to improve poor people's lives."[8] Participants at the 1999 and 2000 conferences concluded that *although some solutions to development problems are high-tech, there are relatively low-tech, simple, and commonsense solutions available for many development challenges.* It is sensible to *weave a development strategy that stresses practical, efficient solutions that are based on available technologies; pays attention to new, emerging, or "over-the-horizon" technologies for their potential positive and negative effects; and concentrates on the needs of the poor.*

> Weave a development strategy that stresses practical, efficient solutions that are based on available technologies; pays attention to new, emerging, or "over-the-horizon" technologies for their potential positive and negative effects; and concentrates on the needs of the poor.

Lessons Learned

Successful integration of technology has demonstrated that the design of and decisions about technology must involve providers and users, so that needs, usability, affordability, and desires (even those based on culture) are taken into account.

In Brazil, refrigerators were generously donated to schools without adequate consultation or instruction to teachers, families, or students on their use or maintenance. The donors did not assess in advance whether individuals would know how to use the refrigerators, whether they met a high-priority need that the community felt was crucially important, or whether they were culturally compatible with the values of the users. The

> **Box 2—What is Appropriate Technology?**
>
> Conference participants agreed that appropriate technology:
>
> - Works in a given situation;
> - Can be high-tech or low-tech, off-the-shelf, or newly developed;
> - Solves a specific problem or is at least an improvement;
> - Can be operated and maintained by local people;
> - Is culturally acceptable;
> - Can be "owned" by the local population, not just imposed;
> - Is economically feasible; and
> - Is sustainable.

new technology required a change in behavior to be effective—for example, children could bring fresh food for lunch and store it, and vaccines could be preserved more effectively. But, the people did not make the change. The refrigerators fell into disrepair and stood empty as an example of the many aid projects that have gone awry because of lack of consultation with local citizens.

On the other hand, electronic community centers called Little Intelligent Communities (LINCOS) were installed as pilot projects in rural communities in Costa Rica by The Foundation for Sustainable Development, with good success to date. (See footnote 1, Box 1.) The technology involved in LINCOS (and similar successful digital centers) is far more "advanced" than that of a refrigerator, but each unit is based on a prototype that is tailored to the needs of the specific community. Initially, the LINCOS unit may be installed for the purpose of providing access to information technology. Eventually, it can be expanded to include banking, radio, telemedicine applications, and water purity testing. The goal of the donors is to empower people to use the technology intelligently for economic and social growth; therefore, the Foundation ensured that the individuals who were going to use it were the driving force in its development. Then they ensured that these individuals had ownership over the technology, knew how to maintain it, and were able to identify additional applications that were needed. LINCOS pilot projects and similar programs have been effective and sustainable—in contrast to the refrigerators.

A consultation process among providers and users, beginning with a list of criteria related to appropriate technology, should be undertaken before funds are committed or a program is initiated to determine whether to proceed. This applies to donors and other providers, national and local governments, and foremost the people who will need to own the technology. To transfer technology successfully, *donors need to ensure that they communicate with elites and poor alike so the technology does not benefit the "ins"*—people who are already advantaged and empowered—*at the expense of the "outs,"* or, worse, that access to the technology is not blocked by the "ins." The principle of good two-way communication applies equally at the international level between developed and developing countries.

> **A consultation process among providers and users should be undertaken before funds are committed or a program is initiated. Donors need to ensure that they communicate with elites and poor alike so the technology does not benefit the "ins" at the expense of the "outs."**

When introduction of a technology or product does not solve a given problem because it is too high-tech or it cannot be culturally absorbed or operated and maintained properly or economically, that failure can set back development, waste resources, and create hostility toward technology and its advocates. Therefore, decision-makers should not become "blinded by science" and jump at each new technological product that comes on the market. Nor should leaders discard the possibility of using a technology solution that is more expensive but might be far more efficient than other solutions. In a world of limited financial resources—especially in developing countries—decisions about how to allocate those resources must be made after careful consideration.

Complexity and Controversy in Choosing Appropriate Technology

Deciding on the appropriate technology is not always a straightforward task. New technology often is very controversial, and its use—and whether or not it is regarded as appropriate—is heavily influenced by cultural, religious, and personal beliefs. This is evident in issues surrounding two crucial problems in development: AIDS and food security.

> **New technology often is very controversial, and its use is heavily influenced by cultural, religious, and personal beliefs.**

Scientific complexity still affects controversial areas of technology integration, such as whether or not genetically modified crops should be integrated into agricultural practices. Lack of consensus about the effects and safety of genetically modified crops has resulted in a polarized situation in which developing countries, developed countries, and environmentalists dispute whether to allow these technologies to be used. *Evaluating and continually updating a comprehensive development strategy infused by technology requires a responsible balancing of factors; consultation among a wide variety of governmental, non-governmental, and private-sector entities; consideration of culture and moral beliefs; attention to economic requirements and consequences; and evaluation of the long-term repercussions of the crises faced and the choices made.*

Technology of Women's Health—Population and HIV/AIDS

Between the years 2000 and 2025, the world's population is expected to increase from 6 billion to 8 billion, and 97% of the new 2 billion people will be born in developing countries. On a much shorter timeline, the number of individuals infected with HIV/AIDS will continue to grow at an alarming rate—as will its devastating effect on quality of life and economic development. Previously unaffected regions of the world are experiencing shocking increases in the rate of infection, including India, China, the Caribbean, Central and Eastern Europe, and parts of Latin America. Today AIDS is the fourth leading cause of death in the world; and in Africa the chances of contracting HIV in one's lifetime are greater than 1 in 3. With statistics such as these, conference participants suggested that the importance of the availability of condoms and continuation of research into alternative methodologies of birth control and HIV/AIDS prevention would be one element of a comprehensive poverty alleviation strategy. *Providing condoms not only affects population growth; it also helps to protect women and their infants from the spread of HIV/AIDS.*

The number of individuals infected with HIV/AIDS will continue to grow at an alarming rate, in parts of the developing world, as will its devastating effect on economic development.

Incorporating contraceptive technology into a strategy for the alleviation of global poverty is complex because of economic, political, and cultural influences on the acceptance of contraceptive technology. For example, overcoming strong cultural barriers that shun the use of contraceptives and relegate women to a subservient role requires active leadership and education, patience, and perseverance. Political pressure that rejects contraceptive measures on a religious or a moral basis also continues to be a limiting factor. The positive benefits of promoting dissemination of contraceptive technology, research into new methods, and ways to improve availability and use, however, point to the need to incorporate and emphasize this sensitive subject in a women's health pillar of a global strategy for poverty reduction.

Food Technology

With the world population continuing to boom, food needs also will continue to increase. The demand for food grains in developing countries is expected to increase 59% in the next 25 years. Therefore, it is particularly worrying that agricultural yields have been declining—the growth rate of cereal yields, for example, has declined from 2.9% per year in 1967-82 to 1.8% in 1982-94.[9] In the 1970s, new agricultural research led to improved maize and the "green revolution"—much higher agricultural yields.

The new green revolution may lie in biotechnology—using living organisms to produce or modify products to improve plants and animals—although the issue is rife with controversy. Advances in biotechnology have led to seeds with greater nutritional value, fruits that over-ripen less frequently, and plants that are more resistant to stresses, such as drought, toxic heavy metals, pests, and diseases. Biotechnology also has improved the quality of meats, animal resistance to diseases, and the efficiency of weight gain in animals. Debate over the use of these genetically modified crops and animals derives from political, social, economic, and ecological questions of biodiversity, safety, and the potential for increasing food security in the developing world. Demonstrable evidence of long-term outcomes on ecological stability, animal and plant viability, and human health remains limited and open to subjective interpretation. This controversy pits the need for lower food costs and increased production against the fears of environmentalists, with developing countries caught in the middle. Indeed, one of the major opinion splits is between the United States and European governments.

> **The new green revolution may lie in biotechnology although the issue is rife with controversy.**

Without a cohesive scientific consensus, the question of who or what institution can provide objective guidance on the safety of such technologies stands as a prominent concern, and the political debates continue. Not only are the scientific results unclear, the economic consequences of the technology for the poor are questioned, because it will enable laboratory-based production of goods grown in tropical regions—thus depriving the poor of their competitive advantage. The potential benefits and, simultaneously, the complexity of the application of biotechnology to the problems of food scarcity and distribution require considerable analysis and strong leadership in order that the advantages can be spread to the poor and rich alike and the integrity of the Earth's biodiversity can be maintained.[10]

Scaling Up What Works

The potential benefits of appropriate technology in poverty alleviation are enormous when technologies proven to meet the needs of the poor and improve their lives reach millions of people. A key problem noted at the conference was how to "scale up" success stories, so that they make a difference at the broad national level. The answer to the question of how to achieve this crucial "scaling up"—in access, multiplication and diffusion, job opportunities, and effectiveness—is fundamental to any strategic use of technology in development.

> **"Scaling up" technology successes to reach millions of people and make a difference at the broad national level is fundamental.**

Conference participants said that two different but intertwined processes are required to overcome constraints, create access to technology, and scale up successes. One relates to "technical" aspects (such as infrastructure, regulatory regime, start-up and management, replication and funding) that are necessary for technology to take root—that is, getting as many people as possible access to technology and related resources that work for them. The other relates to the "human" elements that are necessary for societies to change and grow, so that they can take greater advantage of new technologies and speed the journey out of poverty. These human elements involve more abstract qualities such as leadership, governance, education, and culture. These technical and human elements reinforce each other. To empower citizens to foster changes in their governance, access to technololgy and related resources, personal circumstances, and national development. The following two sections concentrate on these two types of elements that are necessary for technology to play a significant role in development.

Fundamental Constraints on Scaling Up Technology

For technology to have an impact on people's lives, people must have access to it. For a variety of reasons, poor people and poor countries around the world simply do not have adequate access to technology that can benefit them. The main factors that slow or restrict the availability and integration of various development-beneficial technologies into poor communities are:

- Lack of strategies and resources in developing countries to acquire, provide access to, and integrate technology for development;
- Lack of a comprehensive international strategy and related resources that make available a broad range of appropriate technology for development;
- Poor governance exacerbated by corruption that creates an unattractive investment climate, hinders connectivity and access to other technologies, restricts the growth of private enterprise and markets, dilutes the effectiveness of foreign assistance, and prevents poor people from having the power to exert pressure for access to technology;
- Lack of resources in developing countries to fight disease and other debilitating conditions that curtail human productivity and life;
- Lack of sufficient education at all levels in most developing countries;
- Cultural resistance to change;
- Lack of meaningful dialogue between developing countries—including their poor people—and donor countries on development needs and priorities.

INCREASING TECHNOLOGY ACCESS, JOBS, AND RESOURCES

Conference participants recommended a strategy that calls for scaling up and diffusing appropriate technology to all people as much as possible, believing firmly that overcoming the obstacles and successfully carrying out such a policy will have significant beneficial effects for economic progress and governance in the medium term.

This chapter leads off with discussion of three technology-related activities that are key to scaling up technology in a poverty-reduction strategy: increasing connectivity; developing more technology-related businesses and jobs to spur economic, social, and middle-class growth; and broader diffusion of lower-technology products that can dramatically improve poor people's lives. Success in these activities will require deliberate actions and cooperative effort by developing country governments and their citizens, the international community, and the private sector—as well as more funding—topics that are covered in the second half of the chapter.

Building Connectivity

Connectivity—by phone or Internet—can enhance the ability of people to improve their quality of life, for example, by being able to reach relatives, a doctor, or an information source. Connectivity also can be the start of a pathway out of poverty, as it improves education, training, and business **Connectivity is productivity.** opportunities, thus making people more informed, productive and competitive. As one conference participant said, "Connectivity is productivity."

New technology has the power to connect people in increasingly rapid ways. Wireless technologies and the declining costs of telecommunications as a result of the switch from copper wires to fiber optics and other advances are enabling more communication worldwide. While the telephone took almost 75 years to reach 50 million users, it took the World Wide Web only 4 years to do so.[11]

Yet developing countries continue to lag far behind developed countries in terms of connectivity—in having the tools one uses to communicate with others. During the conference, for example, participants noted that by the late 1990s, 42% of the world's people age 15 and over had never made a phone call. The average high-income country has roughly 8 times the per capita purchasing power of a South Asian country, but it has 107 times as many computers, 265 times as many mobile phones, and 3,531 times as many Internet hosts.[12]

There are many reasons to fear that the connectivity gap will not be closed anytime soon. Principal among them is that *developing countries do not have the infrastructure—human and physical—that is necessary to support telecommunications*

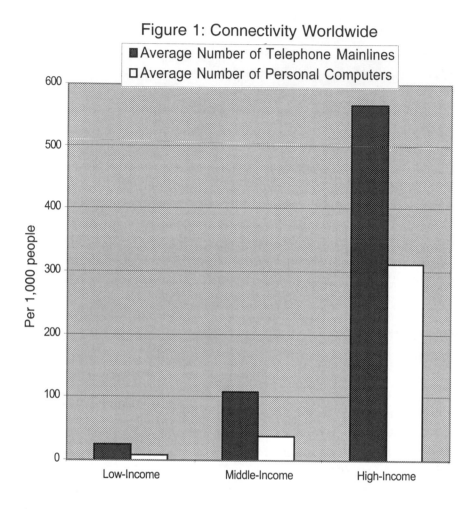

Figure 1: Connectivity Worldwide

Source: International Telecommunication Union (ITU), *World Telecommunication Development Report 1999* (Geneva: ITU, 1999).

technology. For example, Organisation for Economic Cooperation and Development (OECD) countries have roughly 17 times as many technicians and 8 times as many scientists per capita as countries of sub-Saharan Africa. Rich countries also have far more telephone lines and personal computers per person than poor countries (see Figure 1).[13]

Technology and innovation are providing several new ways for people in poor areas without phone lines or electricity to have access to phones and the Internet. Some examples are:

Electronic community centers – The electronic community center is an excellent example of increasing connectivity without huge infrastructure investment. LINCOS (see preceding section) and similar projects, such as Greenstar, are highly successful prototypes that bring connectivity and opportunity to people in poor, rural, villages by providing a simple community-run, satellite-linked telecommunications center. Capabilities include e-mail, education and information, e-commerce, telemedicine, phoning, faxing, and water testing or purification. LINCOS is set up in refurbished shipping containers. Greenstar and LINCOS are both solar-powered stand-alone centers costing about US$100,000 each.

> **The electronic community center is an excellent example of increasing connectivity without huge infrastructure investment.**

Cell phones – Another example of a connectivity project is GrameenPhone, with its goal of one cell phone per village in Bangladesh purchased with microloans of approximately US$200. Each month the program adds 100-200 new villages. To date, this project has resulted in connectivity for approximately 3,000 villages with an average of 2,000 people in each, providing more than 6 million people with access to doctors, job opportunities, relatives, and market prices.

Satellites – New advances in satellite connectivity can overcome part of the infrastructure shortcomings that obstruct connectivity. In the past, fiber cables required for connection were available only in major cities. That has changed, and whole areas that previously were without telephone or Internet access can connect because satellites can bring the Internet to sites in remote areas. Successful deployment of this technology is a major development with much promise for applications that will greatly benefit the rural poor.

Many developing countries cannot take advantage of satellites right overhead, though, because *often governments have policies in place that act as barriers to connectivity being a reality,* as Santiago Ontañón pointed out in his conference remarks. *The problem is removing the regulatory and other barriers so that ordinary people can have the equipment and the necessary access to connect.* This will take action by national governments, as described in the next chapter.

> **The problem is removing the regulatory and other barriers so that ordinary people can have the equipment and the necessary access to connect.**

Scaling Up Tech-Related Businesses and Creating Jobs

Technology has proven itself to be a job creator in both the old economy and the new economy. Building up the private commercial sector to take advantage of technology, bring new technology and services into the country, generate jobs, and boost productivity is a necessary part of a poverty-reduction strategy. This is especially true because these activities help build the crucially important middle class.

Technology Centers

The challenge is to multiply successes that can create jobs and build a middle class and to spread the benefits beyond isolated pockets of success.

Perhaps the best new economy example is the creation of pockets of high-technology activity, such as in Bangalore, India, where microchip and software manufacturing thrive. Or consider Ireland, where an impressively successful Internet service economy is far removed from its customers. The challenge is to multiply these kinds of successes that can create jobs and build a middle class and to spread the benefits beyond isolated pockets of success. *This broader success requires governments to generate the business-friendly environment, infrastructure, and incentives that bring domestic and international investment.* (See Box 7 on page 55)

Small and Medium-Size Businesses

Small and medium-size businesses are key to creating the jobs and the economic and social momentum that build a middle class. Building a busi-

Small and medium-size indigenous businesses that draw on technology for improved products or facilitate access to technology by a broader sector of society are crucial to development.

ness requires an entrepreneur to have seed money, capital, knowledge, management skills, trained workers, and more. In poor developing countries, it is particularly daunting to acquire these tools, *but small and medium indigenous businesses that draw on technology for improved products or facilitate access to technology by a broader sector of society are crucial to development.*

Developing country governments need to use actions and resources to encourage entrepreneurs to build new enterprises. The world community should place greater emphasis on funding, training, and information.

The U.S. non-profit organization EnterpriseWorks Worldwide promotes social and economic growth around the world by operating on the philosophy of "fighting poverty with profit." EnterpriseWorks provides comprehensive business development services (BDS) to small and medium-size businesses. For example, EnterpriseWorks is developing a website that focuses on West African sesame production and sales to help make buyer-seller connections between small-scale Malian farmers and international sesame buyers. The site also would also provide a timely and authoritative source for information on prices and trends in the world sesame market and for African sesame in particular. As more and more people are empowered, they can collectively transform their local communities.

EnterpriseWorks has used information technology to create a new tool that should enable successful start-up of thousands of new developing-world businesses. EnterpriseSearch is a powerful, first-of-its-kind, small-enterprise/sustainable development search engine for the Worldwide Web. It is designed to help developing-world entrepreneurs and producer associations, development specialists, local and multinational businesses, and program funders easily locate information on enterprise development and related issues. The search engine indexes and updates its 12,000 project reports, articles, lessons learned, and personal success stories from 60 bilateral agencies, multilateral institutions and development banks, foundations, and non-governmental development organizations in multiple languages, including English, French, and Spanish.[14]

Microenterprise

At the individual and village level, the positive effect of Internet technology and connectivity on society and its ability to "scale up" best practices is evident in microfinance, as Jacques Attali, President of PlaNet Finance,[15] explained in his conference remarks. One by one, millions of people in developing countries have created income for themselves and their families since the 1970s with loans ranging from US$50 to several hundred dollars to establish self-employment projects, such as by purchasing a cow, a loom, a sewing machine, or a cell phone. In addition to economic and social benefits—including greater empowerment for women and their children—these new microenterprises can contribute to strengthening local civil society.

Linking the Internet to microfinance institutions and to commercial lenders and potential lenders employs technology to scale up a poverty-reduction method (microcredit) that has been proven to achieve its goals. Microfinance operates in many places where connectivity is low, but even marginal connectivity improves microfinance. For example, the Internet can quicken the exchange of information among microfinance entities, aid in off-line and on-line training, and link microfinance institutions to the broader financial markets of the world so that they have more access to funding. It has been estimated that the current 16 million microloans worldwide could be multiplied to 100 million microloans—reaching the world's poorest families over the next few years with US$20 billion in commercial funding.[16]

> **Linking the Internet to microfinance institutions and to commercial lenders and potential lenders employs technology to scale up a poverty-reduction method (microcredit) that has been proven to achieve its goals.**

Broadening Access to Lower-Technology Products

Small, relatively low-tech products and processes can have huge effects in improving the quality of life. The challenge is to scale them up to reach greatly increased numbers of people. Of course, some of the most important examples are vaccines, medicines, and simple items like filter cloths and mosquito nets to prevent and control deadly diseases. Several other very dif-

> **Small, relatively low-tech products and processes can have huge effects in improving the quality of life.**

ferent examples that were given in the conference are described below, and Box 3 gives additional examples of technology that can be very effectively scaled up.

Water purification – Solar-powered systems can disinfect drinking water with ultra-violet (UV) rays. One device, called UV Waterworks, can supply 1,000 villagers with safe water for a year for only US$0.05 per person. The machine costs US$1500. This invention has enormous potential for saving lives that otherwise would be lost to water-borne disease, a major cause of death in the developing world.[17]

Condoms and family planning education – Condoms and family planning education are low-tech items, but they are very important in terms of their

---

Box 3—Some Projects That Scale Up Technology*

- *Satellites* can connect previously unreachable people to telephones and the Internet for economic, social, and political growth.

- *Electronic community centers* provide villagers with Internet and phone connectivity, along with the hardware for business, education, health information, and cultural preservation.
  - Cost: The LINCOS version costs US$100,000 each to serve a village of 3,000. Greenstar costs approximately the same amount.

- *Cell phones* in rural villages provide connectivity and income.
  - Cost: US$125 million initial funding to establish GrameenPhone in Bangladesh.
  - Cost: US$200 to purchase each phone; income from phones pays operating costs.

- *Technology-based small and medium-size businesses* create jobs that help build economic growth and middle classes. More capital and business training is needed.
  - *Local processing of coffee* boosts incomes of small-scale farmers 30-50% and creates hundreds of jobs.
    - Cost: US$40,000 per facility.
  - *Manufacture and sale of manual water pumps* for irrigation strengthens local manufacturing capacity and increases productivity, crop yields, and incomes. In West Africa, 6,000 pumps have been sold, adding US$12 million in new income.
    - Cost: US$100 per pump generates US$2,000 added income over the 6-year life of the pump; 10,000 pumps would generate US$20 million added income for small-scale farmers, plus profits for pump manufacturers.

- *Biomass and charcoal clean-burning stoves* improve quality of life and decrease environmental degradation.
  - Cost: US$4-20 per household stove.
  - Cost: US$100,000 to "adopt a village" and set up stove production

- *Solar-powered water purification devices* produce life-saving clean drinking water for pennies per year after acquisition cost of about US$1500 each.

*Where costs are given, they are investment costs and do not include all operating costs unless specified.

impact on women's health, in decreasing or spreading out pregnancies, and in reducing the incidence of HIV/AIDS for women and their babies.

Efficient stoves – The turbo-stove being introduced into China and Brazil is an efficient stove that burns wood and biomass, a renewable energy source. It is a healthy and environmentally clean technology, consuming one-sixth the fuel that people consume today in their agricultural communities around the world. Each stove costs just US$20. Varying versions of it are in use in other poor regions, having been adapted to local conditions. At a cost of $4-8 per stove, EnterpriseWorks has facilitated the sale of more than 100,000 fuel-efficient charcoal stoves in Benin, Mali, and Senegal, providing training and intensive marketing assistance to help private-sector manufacturers build a customer base and ensure long-term profitability and sustainability. Stove-using families have saved more than US$13 million in fuel costs, typically halving the amount they spend on charcoal and deforestation, and emissions of carbon dioxide have been reduced significantly. These stoves have a sensible cost and clear advantages for people and the environment; the question is how to make these and similar stoves available to millions of people—how to "scale" up.

The best way to scale up these kinds of programs is for governments, foundations, corporations, philanthropists, and others to link into technology projects that are known to work and to donate financial and/or in-kind assistance to spread the product to more poor areas and people. A creative proposal related to the stoves, which goes beyond donating and shipping them to their new owners, is to "Adopt a Village" and create a capacity to manufacture the stoves there to supply a larger area. (See Helena Chum's conference paper on pages 135-136 for the stoves proposal and a broader discussion of renewable energy technologies.)

The best way to scale up low-technology projects is to donate financial and/or in-kind assistance to spread the product to more poor areas and people.

The Role of Governments and Citizens in Developing Countries

Governments of developing countries are central in transitioning their countries and people through national development, and this is especially true in the midst of globalization and the Technology Revolution. The governments have responsibility for their people. Thus, in terms of development, governments should emphasize improving the human condition, especially through healthcare and education programs. They also must govern in a way that creates conditions leading to access to technology, equitable growth, and reduction of poverty. Citizens can be crucial in this effort, in pushing their governments to act and also acting on their own.

Governments of developing countries must govern in a way that creates conditions leading to access to technology, equitable growth, and reduction of poverty. Citizens can be crucial in this effort, in pushing their governments to act and also acting on their own.

Improving the Climate for Foreign Investment and Competition

Private international capital flows are pivotal in attracting new technologies that can fuel development in poor countries. To effectively compete for and attract

Governments and their people need to know what steps they should take to integrate technology and make it available to all.

these investment funds, a developing country government must take the steps required to create a stable environment characterized by the rule of law, transparency, lack of corruption, social justice, strong institutions, and other elements of good governance. Also important to the investment climate are deregulation and reasonably minimal bureaucracy. Finally, *governments* must be aware of the benefits and drawbacks of various technologies and, importantly, they also *need to know what steps they should take to integrate technology and make it available to their citizens. The public needs to know too so the government can be held accountable.*

In the case of telecommunications, among the most important steps a government can take to maximize the availability and usefulness of new technology is to prudentially privatize and deregulate the

The World Bank estimates that there are 28 million people—almost all of them in developing countries—who are on waiting lists for telephone installation, largely because of inefficient state monopolies and regulatory regimes.

telecommunications industry. One participant mentioned that in Mexico a person must get numerous permits to obtain a domain name for his or her website. The World Bank estimates that there are 28 million people—almost all of them in developing countries—who are on waiting lists for telephone installation, largely because of inefficient state monopolies and regulatory regimes.[18]

The way to alleviate these problems is to create a better telecommunications policy environment. A recent study suggests that the combination of privatization, good regulation, and a competitive mobile phone market could double the number of phone lines per capita in some of the poorer markets in Africa.[19] Progress along these lines has been slow, however. More than 90 developing countries opened their telecommunications sector to private participation between 1990 and 1998 (with US$214 billion in new investments committed).[20] Yet data from the International Telecommunication Union suggests that only 12% of local markets in developing countries are liberalized in this way.[21]

The development of Internet Service Providers (ISPs) in Brazil is one example of how creating a better telecommunications environment can bring power and progress to citizens. In the early 1990s, the Ministry of Science and Technology argued successfully that the Internet is not "telecommunications" and therefore should not be a part of the government-controlled telecommunications monopoly. This resulted in an explosion of ISPs and contributed to a 24% compound annual growth rate in the information and communications technology (ICT) sector between 1997 and 2001. Not only did this generate new wealth, increase accessibility, and improve connectivity; it also promoted support for the liberalization of basic telecommunications.[7]

Indeed, fostering of competition is just as important as deregulation. Conference participants pointed out that the privatization experience in some Eastern European countries had gone wrong because of insufficient efforts to promote competition. In many countries around the world, subsidies for huge telecommunications companies drown out competition and keep prices artificially high. One study showed that in Africa the cost of accessing the Internet was 700% higher in countries with the least open telecommunications regimes than in the countries with the most open telecommunications regimes.[22] *It is critical, therefore, that governments take the necessary steps to enact policies that will foster competitive private-sector activity.*

One study showed that in Africa the cost of accessing the Internet was 700% higher in countries with the least open telecommunications regimes than in the countries with the most open telecommunications regimes. It is critical, therefore, that governments take the necessary steps to enact policies that will foster competitive private-sector activity.

The Role of the International Community

The international community often has been unsuccessful in its attempts to "help" developing countries. An important reason has been its failure *to encourage participation and ownership by citizens at all economic and social levels in specific development programs and projects to reach down and include the grassroots.* Encouraging this participation is essential in future efforts. One reason is that economic policy, and often reform, tend to benefit the "ins" at the expense of the "outs"—that is, people who are in the government or close to it benefit at the expense of those who are outside of the government process. *If all of society is to reap the benefits of progress, more people have to participate in the governing process and hold the government accountable.*

How can the international community encourage this? One way is to provide tools that enable ordinary citizens to serve as "watchdogs" over their government. One example, discussed at the conference, is to encourage deregulation and the other reforms by providing a template that lays out what countries must do to make telecommunications industries most effective for the people. This template would cover steps that governments must take to achieve full connectivity in the country—and the dilemmas they are likely to encounter during the process. While there would be many steps that would be country-specific, a template of necessary steps in the abstract might be helpful to countries that are farthest behind. The elements would include privatization, removal of some subsidies, consistent standards, reasonable permit requirements, and less overall bureaucracy. In particular, publication of such a template could help citizens to monitor the progress their government is making and to lobby more effectively for change. Work

along these lines is underway now on several fronts as the Group of 8 industrialized states(G8), G-15 developing states, the World Bank, and other
organizations increase their focus on closing the digital divide.(See endnote
1.)

Donor Assistance

Of course, one of the most important roles of the international community is financial assistance. Yet, even if governments of poor countries take
steps to improve governance, liberalize their economies, and set up sound
regulatory frameworks, they will continue to lack adequate resources to build
up infrastructure and take advantage of new technologies. Governmental and
institutional international financial resources for development are woefully
inadequate. In 1999, donors gave only 0.22% of their gross national product
(GNP) as official development assistance (the UN target is 0.7%).[23] Even
worse, aid declined during the 1990s—in real terms and as a share of GNP—
until the Asian financial crisis provoked additional aid. Sixteen of the 21
major aid donors spent a smaller share of their GNP on development assistance during 1997-98 than during 1988-92.[24] Government foreign aid budgets
need to increase, at least during this transition period of
the ongoing Technology Revolution and spreading globalization. Specifically, *conference participants strongly recommended that donors increase their development assistance generally, and in particular increase their development funding to technology-driven programs in a wide range of technologies and related policy reform to multiply successful models and increase access.*
Specific programs can include, for example, distance learning   and   necessary   equipment;   purchase   and
distribution/set up of energy-efficient stoves, water purifiers, and electronic
community centers; seed money or loans for micro, small, and medium-sized
technology-related businesses; business management training; funding to
enhance research capabilities at developing country universities; and energy
infrastructure. More detail is on page 66.

**Donors should
increase their devel-
opment assistance
and especially fund-
ing for technology-
related reforms and
projects.**

Developing Country Models – As a subset of donor assistance, conference
participants noted, the least-developed countries need to work with developing-country role models rather than less-relevant industrialized country models. One model that works well involves an industrialized country funding a
project that involves two developing countries at different stages of development—for example, as Japan has done.

The Private Sector Role

The private sector also must play its part in development. Bill Joy estimated at the conference that new technologies will create trillions of dollars

of new wealth over the next 50 years. Some of this money should be directed toward enabling less fortunate people of the world to benefit from the
new wealth and these technologies—not only for moral
reasons but also to increase customer bases in developing
countries. First and foremost, investment must be spread
to the poorest countries, which are now left out of these
flows that are crucial to development. As suggested above,
commercial funding of microcredit loans could increase
substantially the resources available to microentrepreneurs in the developing world. Medical research and some subsidized drugs
already are combating debilitating disease, but much more must be done in
medical care and other sectors, including water, the environment, and agriculture.

> **Some of the wealth of the Technology Revolution should be directed to enabling less fortunate people to benefit.**

Another initiative suggested at the conference, which met with some
support from participants and bears further investigation, is a small and
medium-size business development bank. This bank could be a hybrid institution capitalized mainly by private sector contributors, but also with funds
from governments. One goal would be to build up the remote markets in
many poor countries. The institution would serve three main functions: to
provide capital to small firms to help them grow; to provide technical assistance in the form of business development services; and to inform foreign
firms about the best ways to invest in remote areas. The focus therefore
would be on funding firms and entrepreneurs directly, rather than giving
money to governments.

The World Bank Information for Development (InfoDev) Program
operates in somewhat the same fashion and for the same purpose, with corporations and governments as funders. It is a global grant program managed by the World Bank to promote innovative projects that use information and communication technologies (ICTs) for economic and social
development, with a special emphasis on the needs of the poor in developing countries. The program funds small pilot projects, such as a non-
governmental organization (NGO) project that transmits medical information to sub-Saharan Africa, with grants of US$250,000-500,000. The funders
are governments and corporations. Some participants suggested that if a
larger program were created in the form of a hybrid bank, the regional
development banks could be involved as well.

Private Sector Investment

Donor aid levels would not be such a serious matter if poor countries
were receiving large amounts of private funding. However, although private
inflows to developing countries have skyrocketed in recent years—to some
$257 billion in 2000 (about 5 times the size of development assistance)—

In 2000, 75% of the $257 billion foreign private investment in the developing world went to 10 countries. It has to be spread more widely to include the poorest countries.

almost three-quarters of foreign direct investment went to 10 developing countries that are better business risks than others.[25] This high level of investment is not being spread to the poorest countries: *it is not trickling down. It is crucial that as developing country governments decrease business risk, for example, by cleaning up corruption and instituting sound policies, private foreign investment must spread more widely into the poorer countries as well.*

Subsidies and Research

Poor countries are unable to afford many of the products, such as large quantities of software, that are protected by the international intellectual property rights regime. This issue recently has received international attention with regard to the availability of AIDS medicine in Africa. Participants recognized that solid proprietary property rights are essential if innovation is to be encouraged. This regime, however, does raise prices and curtail access to new technology in poor countries. One option may be to set up an international fund that subsidizes countries or small and medium-size enterprises to give them access to the expensive goods, such as essential new medicines or important inputs into industry. Other possibilities are intergovernmental arrangements that provide subsidies for poorer countries to purchase certain technology, including computers and software, or direct subsidies to poor countries wherein private sector concerns accept a lower price for their goods.

Development of HIV/AIDS drugs continues to be a prominent area of research and development (R&D) for the pharmaceutical industry. Manufacture and distribution of HIV/AIDS drugs has become a dynamic, controversial point of disagreement between developed and developing countries and the pharmaceutical industry. There is no simple solution; the interests of the private and public sectors do not coincide, and concrete evidence of all the consequences of a given plan of action is not possible, making a clear decision impossible. In particular, the long-term effect of selling HIV/AIDS drugs at or below cost, or at little profit, on future R&D is unclear. Some observers argue that drug companies will have reduced incentive to continue to research other diseases that are endemic in developing countries if they fear they will not be able to recoup their investments because of the HIV/AIDS precedent. Others focus their arguments on the sanctity of intellectual property rights and patent law, wishing to contain the manufacture of generic drugs. Regardless of what arguments are made, however, there are humans who are dying and drugs that increase the quality and length of life, and many people who feel that should be the sole consideration.

In a promising development, after months of effort, a public/private sector global coalition is initiating an aggressive plan to purchase drugs to treat HIV/AIDS at cost from pharmaceutical companies and to expand prevention projects. Facilitated by UN agencies, the intention is to raise US$6 billion a year or more from government sources. A portion of the money also would be dedicated to malaria and tuberculosis treatment.[26] Major philanthropic support of drug and vaccine research and distribution by the Bill and Melinda Gates Foundation also sets an outstanding example. While hugely commendable, these efforts are not sufficient. *Continued drug R&D and distribution efforts are suitable candidates for conscious earmarking of the expected new wealth generated within the private sector by the Technology Revolution.*

Continued drug R&D and distribution efforts are suitable candidates for conscious earmarking of the expected new wealth generated within the private sector by the Technology Revolution

CREATING VIRTUOUS CIRCLES: THE HUMAN ELEMENT

Other elements that are necessary for scaling up the effect of technology lie more in the human realm. They are abstract but extremely important influences, such as political leadership, culture, and human capital (e.g., the education level of a society). In fact, such influences affect not only the application of technology, but also the broader processes of economic and human development. Effecting change in these influences is a complex process. Interestingly, however, not only is technology affected by these characteristics of society, but technology can affect them.

In particular, *technology has the power to help turn vicious circles into virtuous ones.* Poor countries often seem to be trapped in cycles that perpetuate poverty. *These vicious circles include corruption,* which in some poor countries infests all levels of government. Because daily life in these countries requires that one give and even take bribes, corruption perpetuates itself. Breaking this cycle of corruption therefore is extremely difficult because the costs to individuals for breaking the cycle—for example, by refusing to pay a bribe—far outweigh any personal benefits they might attain. Vicious cycles such as this exist in many areas of life in developing countries, from politics to economics to society and culture.

Technological change can enable citizens and governments to alter these dynamics in their countries—in ways that were unavailable previously. In this way, technology not only affects the lives of many individuals, but it has the potential to break the vicious circles and create virtuous ones that contribute to the much-needed changes at the broader national level. These changes are necessary not only for development and poverty reduction but also for scaling up of technological best practices in society.

This section looks at three different circles: leadership, governance, and empowerment; education and migration; and culture and the advancement of technology for progress.

Leadership, Governance, and Empowerment

Of all the instruments that could make or break the vision of poverty being eradicated within 50 years, political leadership is perhaps the most powerful—or potentially the most devastating. Leadership and good governance are now accepted as key ingredients in successful development. For example, effective and visionary leaders have been crucial in the remarkable development history of East Asia, and they have been notably absent in most of Africa.[27] There are exceptions, of course, such as the leadership in Senegal and Uganda, where the spread of HIV/AIDS has been successfully slowed. Thailand has

Of all the instruments that could make or break the vision of poverty being eradicated within 50 years, political leadership is perhaps the most powerful—or potentially the most devastating.

used similar methods, demonstrating that although the three countries are dissimilar culturally, politically, and geographically, the common denominator of strong, active leadership results in crucial advances in development. All three have leaders who have communicated on radio and television and in public appearances how HIV/AIDS is transmitted and what one must do to prevent it.

The consensus that leadership and good governance are essential to development has led development institutions to focus on issues of politics. Notably the World Bank's *World Development Report 2000/2001: Attacking Poverty put political "empowerment" of poor people on equal footing with expanding their economic opportunities and reducing their economic and health risks as tools to fight poverty.*[28]

The problem is that in many countries there is a cycle of repression and political exclusion that not only characterizes poor leadership, but makes it unlikely that citizens will be able to challenge it. It is necessary to change this cycle into one of citizen demand and political responsiveness.

Information technology can empower people who are outside the channels of politics, giving them knowledge and voice to promote change.

Technology can help significantly in this empowerment. As Box 4 highlights, many examples of the power of technology to influence politics to improve governance already exist. In his conference paper, Iqbal Quadir describes how information technology can empower people who are outside the channels of politics, giving them knowledge and voice to promote change. He notes five ways in which technology affects politics:

- Connected people can more easily and efficiently organize themselves.
- Multiple sources of information reduce the chances of people being deceived.
- As private companies increasingly adopt digital technologies and provide efficient services, archaic government processes appear increasingly incompetent—thereby creating pressure for change.
- Seeing how people in other countries live makes people demand fairer and better treatment at home.
- If people are connected across borders, it is more difficult for regimes to demonize foreign peoples.[29]

An argument can be made that technology mixed with political decentralization led to the empowerment of relatively ordinary citizens in Europe in the Middle Ages and afterward—laying the foundation for that continent's economic progress.[30] Merchants emerged with the help of technological innovations such as the water mill, eyeglasses, and mechanical clocks; and with their newfound economic and political voice they pressed for property rights and the rule of law. When those rights and laws were instituted, people benefited from increased freedom and economic progress. Quadir argues that this

---

Box 4—Technology Empowers Citizens

Here are two recent examples of how relatively simple technology can lead to serious political input.

"In Iran, where services have more than doubled since 1990, the telephone was pivotal in the stunning upset victory in May [1997] of moderate president Mohammed Khatami over a hardliner staunchly supported by the political and media establishment. Enthusiasm generated by word of mouth during the 12-day campaign brought millions of Iranians to the polls who had never voted before—particularly women and young people, who rely heavily on telephones because of limited public forums for communications."
–Robin Wright, *Los Angeles Times*, November 10, 1997

"[Chinese] state constraints [on the Internet] are powerful, but not comprehensive. The government felt angry but foolish when, in April last year, 10,000 or more followers of the Falun Gong suddenly surrounded the compound in Beijing where the top leaders live. The gathering had been organized in large part by e-mail that the government could not detect."

–The Economist, July 22, 2000

---

kind of virtuous circle of good governance could come about in today's poor countries through an analogous process.

If more responsive leadership indeed is the result of technological advances, ideally there should be a "feedback" effect, with governments using technology to promote development initiatives. This is how a virtuous circle can be created. The government of Uganda, for example, used basic technology to help break a cycle of corruption (see Box 5). Another use for technology is to communicate better with citizens, explaining the goals of certain policies and explaining government services. Indeed, one confer-

---

Box 5—How Technology Helped Fight Corruption in Uganda

One of the many debilitating effects of corruption is that it prevents government resources from reaching the intended beneficiaries to which they are allotted. In Uganda, a study found that on average less than 30% of the intended non-salary public spending on primary education actually was reaching the schools. The reason, it was assumed, was corruption in the pipeline between the central government and the schools. Relatively simple technology solved the problem: the radio and print media. By making regular announcements in local newspapers and on the radio about how much money was being transferred to districts, the government was able to empower local people to monitor whether the resources arrived. As a result, a follow-up study showed that four years later schools were receiving close to 100% of non-salary public funding.[31]

---

ence participant said that such communication can create much-needed national cohesion in many states that lack it, particularly in Africa.

Building Policy Networks for Development

Empowerment of individuals is happening at the international level too, as NGOs and citizens link up to form coalitions to influence policy. They work with different sectors of society, such as government and business, to form "policy networks." Information technology assists in their ability to highlight differing outlooks on a problem, gather more support, and influence international politics in unprecedented ways.[32] One example is the International Campaign to Ban Landmines, which brings together more than 1,300 groups in more than 90 countries who work locally to internationally to ban antipersonnel landmines.[33] Another example highlighted at the conference was the World Commission on Dams, an independent body representing public, private, and civil society sectors and diverse viewpoints. It was established by opponents and advocates of large dams to assist decision making about dams.[34] Participants applauded these undertakings and hoped that other networks would continue to form, particularly endorsing the development of a network around women's health issues, in part because of the potential benefit to economic development.

Education, Migration, and a New Look at the Brain Drain

It is universally accepted that education is fundamental to the development process. From the empowerment of each individual person to the learning that must take place by governments, education is a *sine qua non* of progress. *No country has ever enjoyed sustained economic progress without literacy rates well in excess of 50%.*[35] Literacy, numeracy, and basic business skills are critical for successful enterprise development—which itself is strategically important for economic development generally and specifically for deploying newer information as well as older off-the-shelf technologies in the effort to eliminate poverty. *There is no question that governments should make education a top priority.*

No country has ever enjoyed sustained economic progress without literacy rates well in excess of 50%.

However, many of the most educated people of poor countries often emigrate to seek better education, employment, and business opportunities. In the short term, this "brain drain" has been very severe: by one estimate, countries in Africa, the Caribbean, Central America, and South Asia have lost as much as one-third of their skilled workers.[36] Although these workers normally send money back home regularly and may pay for siblings' educations, the home countries lose the larger economic value that those workers would create there. Often, those workers are the potential leaders of society that poor countries so desperately need. Likewise, many of the students from developing countries who do their university studies in the United States and other developed countries do not return home after they complete their education.

The brain drain has been long been lamented as a significant problem for developing countries. At this conference, however, a modified view emerged that identified some positive, as well as negative, dimensions of the brain drain as technology begins to change some of the dynamics at work.

Education

Technology can help improve basic and higher education and may even mobilize the private sector to provide some of it through distance education. A recent report for the World Bank concludes that there is high unmet demand for quality distance education in developing countries, especially in Africa.[37] Box 6 discusses how the African Virtual University has been successful in meeting some of this demand. The report notes that this success suggests that "there are potentially profitable returns to be earned by serving these markets. What is needed are *new international and developing-country venture capital funds to invest in these profitable ventures and to help them grow to the point where they can attract more conventional kinds of equity and loan capital.*"

> **New venture capital funds are needed to invest in education.**

A strong and growing university research base is a valuable asset in restoring universities, advancing national development, and retaining talented nationals in poor countries. Research in virtually every sector can be useful and can build national expertise. The challenge is to acquire the funding to build it up.

> **Research in virtually every sector can be useful and can build national expertise. The challenge is to acquire the funding to build it up.**

Box 6—The African Virtual University

The African Virtual University, headquartered in Nairobi, actually is a network of universities; a local institution is competitively selected in every participating country.[38] The local institution provides the necessary equipment (hardware and software), registers students, supervises the study programs, and awards local course credit. The university beams to students via satellite a range of classes, all taught by experts from around the world. Since the project's launch in 1997, 12,000 students in 15 African countries have completed semester-long courses in engineering and the sciences, and more than 2,500 professionals have attended executive and professional management seminars on topics such as, e-commerce, entrepreneurship, and strategy and innovation. In addition, the African Virtual University provides students with access to an online digital library with more than 1,000 full-text journals. Conference participants hoped that this project would provide an example for other initiatives that could help meet the huge demand for education in poor countries.

The African Virtual University, building up university research departments, and other initiatives strengthen higher education in developing countries and help create an environment in which higher education is valued, which in turn enhances a nation's development potential and leadership pool. This is a virtuous circle in itself, as numbers of intellectual elites grow, civil society strengthens, governance improves, emigration declines, and the improved environment begins to bring some expatriates home.

Brain Drain

As technology fosters education, it also can lessen some of the effects of brain drain and general emigration. The Internet and other communication technologies make brain drain migration itself a less severe problem because the technologies render distance less significant. Links between emigrants and their friends and family back home have always been maintained, and that connection is easier now. These links already have their own significant economic benefit: foreign workers send back at least US$75 billion to their home countries each year.

> **As technology fosters education, it also can lessen some of the effects of brain drain and general emigration.**

These remittances are about 50% more than countries receive in development assistance.[39] In fact, the links can have their own direct educational benefit as well: one conference participant told of a taxi driver he had met in New York City who was sending money to his Indian village to start a girls' school.

Technology also can make it less necessary for talented people to leave their countries in the first place. For example, many highly trained Indian nationals work in Bangalore and other cities in India, and "telecommute" to high-tech jobs in developed countries since the area became the Silicon Valley of India. In this way, technology may slow some of the brain drain. It would do so more rapidly if governments were to take appropriate steps to foster a healthy business and overall environment. Many conference participants from developing countries argued strongly that expatriates would want to stay in their home countries or return home if conducive conditions and opportunities existed. When

> **Many conference participants from developing countries argued strongly that expatriates would want to stay in their home countries or return home if conducive conditions and opportunities existed.**

they do return, they bring business knowledge, financial resources, and contacts. Evidence is provided by the story of Infosys, a highly successful technology firm in India (Box 7).

Discussion exploring the impact of technology on the brain drain yielded several intriguing questions: At what stage of development and in what timeframe does one measure the effect of the brain drain? How does one measure the overall gain or loss from the brain drain if 1,000 highly edu-

---

Box 7—A Virtuous Circle Between Infosys and India

In the 1980s, a group of Indian computer experts set up Infosys Technology but found the bureaucracy and lack of infrastructure in India to be overwhelming—it took them 18 months to get a license to set up the company.[40] Therefore, the best way for them to do business was to send people overseas to work with clients, rather than doing the work at home.

In 1991, however, the Indian government began to liberalize the economy and set up a technology park in Bangalore, complete with tax holidays and high-speed satellite links. Infosys therefore could serve its global customers 24 hours a day, 7 days a week, and there was no need to do most of the work anywhere but in India. Today, Infosys is valued at US$16.9 billion and is a leader in India in encouraging private sector responsibility, from paying taxes to contributing to health and education services. It donates 1.25% of its net profits (and plans to raise that ratio to 5%) to the Infosys Foundation, which builds orphanages, schools, libraries, and medical facilities for India's poor people. This is what a virtuous circle could look like.

---

cated or trained people leave a country and one returns to establish a US$1billion dollar company? Does one analyze the effects nationally, regionally, or globally? The answers to these questions are highly debatable, but however one values brain drain, it is apparent that technology may have the ability to lessen its negative effects.

Creating Networks

Networks that are enabled by technology can help to improve education and minimize the effects of brain drain. *Networks or partnerships that link universities, businesses, and communities are key in developing the potential of education in promoting national development.* The 1999 Aspen Institute poverty conference recommended a new international higher education strategy that is based on such partnerships and cooperation to link untapped resources, especially in the private sector.[41] The 2000 conference agreed and especially reiterated *an emphasis on promoting more funding for research in developing country universities to help revitalize them.* In Costa Rica, university research and investigation funds are coordinated through a high technology national center that networks the university systems. More links should be set up between universities in different countries, especially poor ones. *South-south learning and cooperation are ever more important,* because many countries are

Networks or partnerships that link universities, businesses, and communities are key in developing the potential of education in promoting national development.

going through the same processes, and *cross-country learning can help prevent repetition of mistakes.*

Despite technology's ameliorative effects, emigration undoubtedly will continue to some degree for the foreseeable future, and steps must be taken

Build networks that include expatriates and their academic and other contacts at home: one idea is creating an internet based "talent bank", linking together a country's nationals who have expertise on various issues.

to ensure that the short-term burden of losing talented people is minimized. One way to do this is to capitalize more on links with expatriates through building networks that include expatriates and their academic and other contacts at home. Facilitating exchange opportunities and sabbaticals maintains and enhances networks and brings ideas and practices home in ways that may be more culturally palatable than when they come directly from outsiders. One conference participant suggested that countries create an electronic "talent bank"—a searchable website linking a country's citizens all over the world who have expertise on various issues. Such a network could provide an invaluable resource for government and business leaders in developing countries.

Culture and Technological Change

Culture plays a powerful role in determining the success of integrating new technology into society. Many conference participants lamented both that culture sometimes seems to impede technological progress and that technological progress often seems to undermine culture. The lessons from the Industrial Revolution likely will hold for *the Technology Revolution* as well. *It will be turbulent and rather long, we will be unable to predict where it will lead,*

How can people accept technology more readily, and use technology to support their culture rather than undermine it?

and it is likely to result in huge cultural changes. Participants worried about a vicious circle in which culture would restrict technological progress by making people hesitant to take on new ways of doing things, and technology inevitably would erode cultural constraints anyway because technology tends to be a homogenizing force. The question underlying much of the discussion was *how people across cultures could accept technology more readily and then use technology to support their culture rather than undermine it.*

Cultural change is a natural process, but it happens at different paces for different peoples. One participant characterized this phenomenon as "cultural flexibility" and said it was interrelated with "technological adaptability." She argued that *villages and countries with high cultural flexibility and high technological adaptability embrace technological improvements.* Populations with low technological adaptability and low cultural flexibility probably would take a longer time to become participants in globalization. External assistance could help these slower-adapting countries with technological inputs, such as renewable energy cooking systems and elements of sustainable agriculture. Literacy and education programs eventually could move them toward higher technological adaptability, from which they could someday move to higher cultural flexibility.

Some conference participants argued that with this progress and the integration of technology there is a danger of "social amnesia," in which the social and intellectual foundations of society would be forgotten. Others, however, argued that as technology mixes with culture, people generally adapt technology to the society, rather than the other way around. This issue was revisited several times during the conference, but Edith Ssempala's conference remarks seemed to suggest a way to help maintain cultural roots as new methods and technologies are brought into society. She and others argued that *the most effective way of providing external assistance is to put the responsibility in the hands of poor people themselves. This strategy also is likely to be the most effective way to integrate technology into cultures.*

Donors and other outsiders involved in technology transfer need to be cognizant and demonstrate respect for the culture and its importance to the society as change nudges its way in.

Poor people need to have ownership of technology through participation in choosing it and designing how it will be used in their particular situation. In any case, *donors or other outsiders who are involved in technology transfer need to be cognizant of cultural issues.* They need to demonstrate understanding and respect for the culture and its importance to the society as change nudges its way in.

One of the hopes of the conference is that technology can play a role in inspiring ordinary people to reach beyond their surroundings. As people learn more, their idea of "the possible" is expanded. If this human inspiration is combined with knowledge, human progress can be accelerated. For example, one participant talked about meeting U.S. students who are graduating from high school and hearing them say they want to start their own businesses. This attitude differs from that of young people in poor developing countries who are not infused with the mantra of entrepreneurship and the possibilities that the "American Dream" imparts to American youth. Improving economic environments, integrating technological change, and educating people about possibilities can change these attitudes, however, and aspirations can rise.

One of the hopes of the conference is that technology can play a role in inspiring ordinary people to reach beyond their surroundings. As living conditions improve and people learn more, their idea of "the possible" is expanded.

Already, people returning home to developing countries after doing business abroad are relating different views of the world and knowledge of business to their fellow citizens—and the same process is happening as more people communicate over the Internet or explore web sites.

Some aspects of culture undoubtedly will change as the process of learning and adaptation takes place. Such is the nature of progress. Although technology is partly to blame for this change, it also can provide ways to preserve culture. For example, the Greenstar Foundation website features the sights and sounds of local culture from its electronic community centers in India and a Palestinian village on the West Bank, near Hebron.[42] The U.S. Library of Congress does something similar with American culture through its "American Memory" website, which preserves U.S. history, photographs, poetry, and even music.[43] Developing-country governments may want to consider doing something similar with their own cultures.

SUMMARY AND RECOMMENDATIONS

Amartya Sen, winner of the 1999 Nobel Prize in Economics, has argued that development should be regarded largely as the expansion of human freedom in its broadest sense.[44] Crucially, he means not only human freedom—political, economic, religious, and civil—as an end but also as a means to that end. Political, economic, and social freedoms reinforce each other in ways that can spell the end of human deprivation.

Technology has the ability to advance these political, economic, and social freedoms, and in so doing, technology from low-tech to high-tech can be a tremendous force for human development. Endless anecdotes exist about how technology has changed the lives of individuals around the world. More important, however—and more difficult—is the "scaling up" of those individual successes so that appropriate technology gets to much larger numbers of poor people to affect the holistic development of entire societies and thus to meet its potential to dramatically reduce poverty.

This Aspen Institute conference sought to identify how to infuse a comprehensive development strategy with technology—a deliberate plan that will require expenditure and redistribution of some of the enormous windfall of knowledge and resources that will result from the Technology Revolution.

Conference participants concluded that there were two principal elements to that scaling up: a technical element and a human element. The technical element consists of proceeding rapidly with getting the benefits of technology to citizens around the world. The human element consists of all of the human influences that affect how technology is used, from leadership to education to culture. Technology is affected by these dynamics but it also can affect them in beneficial ways. In particular, it has the ability to transform the vicious circles (such as corruption) that seem to trap countries in poverty and instead create or contribute to virtuous circles, such as good governance, that lead up the path of development.

Success in these elements will require action and cooperation by many different actors, including government, the private sector, and civil society. Several important principles and specific recommendations emerged from the conference.

Principles for a Successful Technology-Infused Development Strategy

A variety of concepts based on practical lessons learned and the potential of technology coalesced at the conference into a list of general principles that are central to a successful, comprehensive technology-pulled development strategy that empowers poor individuals and countries to escape poverty. These general principles apply at the international, national, and local levels of governments, the private sector, and civil society.

Seek and apply solutions to problems that especially afflict the poor. The world's poor live primarily in regions that are most prone to disease, malnutrition and famine, the effects of global warming, and environmental degradation that are found less in richer areas. Finding and applying appropriate technological solutions requires extra effort and resources by governments, the private sector, and universities.

Promote access to technology. Poor people must have access to technology that can mitigate or solve problems of poverty and be able to use it to work toward their own solutions. The benefits of technology must be made accessible to far greater numbers of the poor and reach all economic and social levels.

Scale up what works. Replicate and multiply what has been proven to work; use successful ventures, processes, and products as templates.

Apply technology tools at two levels: improving the basics and boosting economic activity. Technology should be used to address basic human needs, such as health and education, and to improve quality of life. Technology also should be used to produce new economic activity. These two mutually reinforcing functions can go on simultaneously, but the former has a stronger moral pull and can help lay the foundation for the latter.

Create an enabling environment. Technology contributes to and benefits from the establishment of a development-enhancing environment that includes an educated and healthy populace, good governance that benefits the people, minimal or no corruption, regulatory structure that fosters competition and transparency, an economic and political system and investment environment that leads to foreign investment and the growth of small and medium-sized as well as larger-scale business enterprises; financial institutions that enable the poor to have access to credit and private property.

Encourage ownership. The most successful approach is a mentality by the user and the user community of being in charge. Donors and developing country governments should not take a patronizing approach to the poor, who can solve many of their own problems if they have basic education, a supportive environment, adequate infrastructure, and the proper tools and are trained to use them.

Use a range of appropriate technology. The benefits of technology are not limited to high-tech satellites and computer systems. Appropriate technology for poverty eradication is technology that works in a given situation, meets a need, is useable and maintainable by local people, is an improvement on the way things have been done in the past, and is sustainable. Low-tech and off-the-shelf solutions, such as netting to protect against malaria from mosquito bites and cloths to filter water, improve lives and make a difference between life and death for millions.

Enable entrepreneurship. Technology should be an outlet and aid to entrepreneurship, in ways such as facilitating microloans and business development services for poor people to assist small and medium-size businesses, especially projects and businesses that introduce or scale up economic and social technology benefits in developing countries. The same is true for larger and more ambitious businesses.

Benefit both the "ins" and the "outs". Technology should not benefit only the "ins"—those people who already are advantaged and empowered. It also should empower the "outs" so that the whole society moves forward. Technology should be available to all of the people who will use it to help to create the all-important middle class.

Improve communication between donors and recipients. Donors must listen and give credence to the needs expressed by lesser-developed countries and to the initiatives they favor. More frequent dialogues should occur on priorities, what works and what helps, and on specific funding. Funding and project priorities and design should reflect joint planning. If donors and developing countries continue to talk past each other, advancement will be impeded.

Respect culture. Culture is crucial in the successful adaptation, use, and sustainment of technology; and its role in slowing or speeding the changes required by technology must be respected. Governments, civil societies, and businesses should work to preserve cultures and the cultural diversity that might be lost in the rush of globalization and the changes that technology brings.

Increase the private-sector role. More developing world private-sector resources are needed in direct investment, technical assistance and training, community support, research, price flexibility, and partnerships. Building and empowering the private sector in developing countries is crucial.

Increase developmental assistance flows and specifically technology-related assistance. Technology-related assistance includes programs that use technology as well as those that enhance access to technology.

Use appropriate development models and maximize information and experience sharing. Developing countries often can learn more from the example of other more-advanced developing countries than from a developed/industrialized country.

Abolish "or" from the language of development and poverty reduction. There is no single magic answer in choosing technologies and approaches. All options should be considered and, ultimately, successful poverty alleviation will incorporate many individuals, ideas, organizations, governments, and approaches. Country strategies need to be more nontraditional and creative. While programs to meet basic needs are being implemented, information and infrastructure technologies as well as job-creation activities need to be funded and put in place.

Recognize that technology is evolving; monitor and act on new developments. The Technology Revolution is ongoing, with benefits, drawbacks, setbacks, inequities, opportunities, ethical issues, and unknowns.

General Recommendations for Players

Enacting these principles requires action, cooperation, and leadership by the major public and private sector players in development: governments, multilateral institutions, corporations, civil society, NGOs and institutions of higher learning, and philanthropists.

Governments and Multilateral Institutions—Action List

Governments of developing and developed countries will be key in facilitating the use of technology for poverty reduction, beginning with providing for basic needs. Developing-country governments have responsibility for their people and for conditions in their country. Only they can provide the regulatory environment and proper incentives for the private sector to act most efficiently in incorporating technology that developed-country governments and multilateral institutions can help make available. Developed countries and multilateral institutions can assist in funding the policy and regulatory reforms and institution-building required to ensure widespread access to technology.

Developing Countries

- *Adopt* a two-part strategy that includes technologies that can improve human conditions and promote growth. This strategy requires being aware of what science and technology can do and how they can be of use to the public.

- *Give* high priority in allocating financial resources to developing human resources—especially health care and universal primary and secondary education, as an educated and healthy populace will be able to take advantage of the opportunities that new technology presents. Also, fund technology-driven change that can speed up community, regional, and national development and entry into the world economy.

- *Institute* sound economic policies and an environment of good governance and rule of law that encourages openess, innovation, and private-sector competition and attracts foreign investment; stop corruption.

- *Be aware of and carry out* steps to integrate technology and make it accessible to all citizens. Streamline regulations and bureaucratic requirements.

- *Build* higher education into a national development asset that advances the country, provides an important research base, retains the best and brightest citizens, and attracts expatriates to return.

- *Offer* incentives to entrepreneurs and businesses of all sizes. Consider creating technology centers such as the one in Bangalore in India.

- *Fund* replications of programs that have worked.

- *Manage* the electromagnetic spectrum and other technology-related public goods to the best development benefit for the country. For example, some countries sell or rent some band width. These proceeds should benefit the whole country.

- *Facilitate* involvement by overseas nationals, utilize their skills, and draw on their resources to promote national development and mitigate the negative impact of the brain drain.

- *Create* other networks to coordinate resources and services available to combat poverty, such as education, health care, and technology information infrastructure.

Developed Countries and Multilateral Institutions

- *Focus* high priority on how best to assist national governments in their fight against poverty, including how technology can be used most effectively in that fight.

- *Communicate* with poor countries and people and listen to their needs and desires.

- *Boost* international aid flows (which have been in decline over the past decade), with particular emphasis on the amount of funding channeled to technology-related development programs, policy reform, and institutional development. (See pages 44 and 66 for more detail).

- **Learn** from technology programs that have worked, and fund multiple similar programs.
- **Partner** with the private sector, including business, NGOs, foundations, and universities.
- **Create** new incentives and subsidies for government and businesses of all sizes in developing countries to access development-related technology.
- **Arrange** programs in which developing countries are models for other developing countries, and facilitate experience-sharing generally.

♠ Corporate Private Sector—Action List

The corporate private sector benefits from advances in new technologies, and enormous amounts of new wealth will be created over the next 50 years. Some sense of morality asserts that wealth should be spread, but so does business sense: as more people participate in growth, there will be more consumers. Business training and philanthropy or reinvestment by corporations in local communities can enhance the business environment, human capital, and overall productivity of the area, to the benefit of the local people and the corporation.

♠ Corporate Private Sector of Developing Countries

- **Seek out** opportunities to promote and help fund human resources programs that drive development, including health, training, and education services for the poor.
- **Pay** taxes.
- **Invest** in local communities; funnel some profits back to the community.
- **Build** supportive relationships with national higher education and training institutions; form partnerships with industrialized country colleges and universities.
- **Fund** replications of projects that have worked.
- **Form** professional associations to strengthen civil society, utilizing communications technology.

♠ Corporate Private Sector of Developed Countries

- **Increase and distribute** investment flows more widely to poor countries as their investment climates improve.
- **Fund** research for problems that are common to poor populations, such as malnutrition and tropical diseases.
- **Subsidize** some technology transfer and the cost of new technology.

- Help *seek* innovative solutions to the problems of poor people.
- *Support* local communities in poor countries through technology, such as providing computers to schools.
- *Engage* in partnerships with developing country higher education institutions.

Civil Society—Action List

Civil society at the national and international levels plays a fundamental role in governance and the adaptation of technology, and its role is being enhanced by new technologies.

Civil Society of Developing Countries

(Citizens, grass-roots groups, media, NGOs, religious institutions, philanthropists, universities, expatriates, interest groups, professional associations)
- *Take advantage* of and build on the benefits of technology (such as enhanced transparency of government and easier communication with others inside and outside the country) that can lead to improved governance and can empower people.
- *Demand* an enabling environment for foreign investment, technology, and entrepreneurship.
- *Create* networks that can influence government decision making to increase access by the society and its poor to technology.

Private Non-corporate/Civil Society of Developed Countries

(NGOs, foundations, individuals, philanthropists, media, universities, religious institutions)
- *Seek out* opportunities to promote and help fund human resources programs that underpin or drive development, including health, training, and education services for the poor.
- *Work* with and directly fund developing country civil society elements, especially by taking advantage of technology.
- *Create or join* networks than can affect economic and political decisions at the international level by linking interest groups within different countries and across borders. Conference participants thought this action would be particularly important in the context of woman's health.

Some Specific Initiatives

Many tasks can be addressed effectively by more than one actor, and often initiatives depend on collaborative approaches across sectors. Several such initiatives were identified in the conference.

Increase Technology-Related Foreign Aid

Governments and multilateral institutions should provide more discretionary foreign assistance funding for technology-related projects in developing countries. It starts with incorporating an "information technology mentality" into all development objectives (from agricultural development to improvements in health service delivery to microenterprise) and ensuring sufficient discretionary resources for these efforts. Such funding should be provided:

- for policy and regulatory reform required to ensure widespread access to and use of technology within countries;
- for promising pilot programs across sectors to encourage innovation
- to replicate successful programs;
- to promote digital opportunities, including exploration of cross-sectoral links to further enhance access to education, to improve the quality of education, and to address the hollowing out of institutions in countries that are hard hit by HIV/AIDS;
- to facilitate and fund projects between less-advanced developing countries and more-advanced developing countries to provide an appropriate model and beneficial practical advice.

Replicate Successful Technology Products and Processes

Corporations, private sponsors, foundations, governments, and institutions should make available to poor countries and people the products or processes that have proven successful in similar circumstances elsewhere. Several examples from this report are electronic community centers, capital and business training for small and medium-size businesses, manual water pumps, solar-powered water purifiers, biomass and charcoal clean-burning stoves—buy the stoves or "adopt a village" and enable it to set up stove production.

Emphasize Women's Health with Research and Technology

Governments and institutions, foundations and NGOs, civil society, researchers, and the private sector all have a role to play in promoting advances in women's health care and helping to make such advances available to all women. Women's health is inextricably tied to the development of a country. Increasing their access to good health facilities, practices, and products can help reduce child mortality, the spread of infectious diseases such as HIV/AIDS, and high birth rates, as well as strengthen their ability to care for their families. Conference participants particularly noted the need for greater use of existing education methods, condoms and more research into alternative contraceptive methods to inhibit the spread of HIV/AIDS and other infectious diseases and reduce high birth rates.

Expand Distance Learning and Develop Language Availability

The private sector, in cooperation with national governments and institutions of higher learning, should continue to develop distance-learning programs that can be used by people in poor and remote areas. This includes voice transcription, Internet programs, and translation into local languages. Poor people absolutely must have access to new knowledge and training if they are to operate effectively in the 21st-century economy. Online digital libraries and support for the education and training of women, in particular, are high priorities.

Establish Professional Associations

Multilateral institutions, journalists, business people, chambers of commerce, and governments can invest in the development of professional associations in developing countries to strengthen civil society and its voice in governance.

Develop National Talent Banks to Assist Development

Governments, NGOs, and corporations should encourage links between their citizens abroad and at home, for example by creating on the Internet a "talent bank" of expatriates who can advise government and business on technology and development. In the past, efforts to educate citizens have been compromised by brain drain (emigration of educated citizens to richer countries), and this type of resource may ameliorate some of the effects of this drain.

Establish University Links and Research

Governments, NGOs, and businesses should encourage links between universities in different countries in an effort to strengthen higher education and promote cross-country learning that enhances the development process and empowers the national elite. This strategy includes "south-south" cooperation between developing countries, as well as "triangular" cooperation, among a rich country, a middle-income country, and a poor country. It is hoped that this cross-country learning would include an examination of the different connectivity programs that have been undertaken in various countries, including the LINCOS electronic community center program in Costa Rica. Research in developing country higher education institutions also should be increased.

Several initiatives were identified for further exploration:

Explore Technology Subsidies - International institutions, the G8, and corporations should explore further the idea of subsidies or a subsidy fund to help developing countries pay the high price of technological advancements that could benefit them but are protected by property rights. Property rights are essential to encourage innovation, but they also make products too costly for many developing countries. Technology subsidies or a subsidy fund that would issue payments to developing countries and small and medium-size enterprises to offset the cost of technology transfer and the use of new technology could alleviate this dilemma.

Explore Template for Connectivity - Public-sector institutions and NGOs could explore whether a "template" for connectivity in developing countries would be useful in providing countries with a guide about the best way to take advantage of IT. The template would explain the deregulation and other steps that are necessary for countries to take in order for telecommunication industries to be most effective and efficient and provide connectivity to the whole society. Such a template could be a useful tool for business and civil society in encouraging their governments to take the required steps.

Explore a Small and Medium-Size Business Development Bank - The public and private sectors could explore the idea of a small and medium-size business development bank within an established institution or as a separate entity. This bank could be capitalized by private-sector contributors, as well as international institutions, such as the World Bank, the International Finance Corporation, and regional development banks. Such a hybrid bank—possibly working through NGOs and the private sector as intermediaries— could help develop the remote markets of poor countries by providing capital to small and medium-size firms and giving them business-related technical assistance. In addition, the bank could inform external investors about the best ways to invest in remote areas. The focus therefore would be on making funding available directly to entrepreneurs and firms, rather than to governments.

Further work should be done on several areas of potential and controversy that are extremely important for poverty reduction, including biotechnology, global warming/climate change, and how to deal with the long term effects of AIDS devastation on societies and economies.

At the root of these actions is a firm belief in the power of individuals and communities to improve their well-being if they are empowered to do so. Deliberate actions are needed to enable the world's poor to thrive in their own social and cultural contexts and expand the depth and breadth of their participation in the world community. Infusing appropriate technology into development through resources, action, and cooperative effort by governments, the private sector, and the civil societies of developed and developing countries can remove the scourge of poverty from the world in the next 50 years. Participants in the "*Alleviating Global Poverty: Technology for Economic and Social Uplift*" conference called on leaders everywhere to supply the critical elements that can make it happen: political will and visionary leadership. .

ENDNOTES

Boxes and Figure

     Box 1—Examples of the Transforming Power of Technology
     Box 2—What is Appropriate Technology?
     Box 3—Some Projects That Scale Up Technology
     Box 4—Technology Empowers Citizens
     Box 5—How Technology Helped Fight Corruption in Uganda
     Box 6—The African Virtual University
     Box 7—A Virtuous Circle Between Infosys and India
     Figure 1—Connectivity Worldwide

a.   James D. Wolfensohn, "Making Globalization Work for the Poor," presented at The Aspen Institute 50th Anniversary Symposium, August 19, 2000. Available at <http://www.aspeninst.org/fifty/wolfensohn.html>

1.   G-8 Summit Declaration, 2000, Okinawa Charter on the Global Information Society, and information on upcoming July 2001 G-8 Summit in Genoa, Italy, at www.library.utoronto.ca/g7. The G-15 Jakarta Declaration, 2001 "focused on bridging the digital divide between the developed and developing worlds and called on multilateral institutions and developed countries to 'encourage and strengthen ICT-related applications and local industry in developing countries' through investment, education and training," World Bank Development News, June 1, 2001. <http://www.worldbank.org/developmentnews

2.   Nancy Bearg Dyke (ed.), *Persistent Poverty in Developing Countries: Determining the Causes and Closing the Gap* (Washington D.C.: Aspen Institute, 1998).

3.   United Nations Development Programme, *Human Development Report 2000: Human Rights and Human Development* (New York: Oxford University Press, 2000).

4.   See case study by Lisa Stosch and Eric Hyman, "The El Salvador Coffee Production and Processing Project of EnterpriseWorks Worldwide" in press, *Business Development Services for Small and Microenterprises* (Ottawa, Canada: International Development Research Centre, 2001).

5.   For example, see the World Bank's Comprehensive Development Framework: <http://www.worldbank.org/cdf/>.

6.   *For further information, see <http://www.peoplink.org/vsouk/>.*

7.   Reed E. Hundt, "The Worldwide Communications Revolution: The Export of the American Idea," in Taylor Boas, *Rapporteur's Report, Global Policy Program,* Carnegie Endowment for International Peace, January 25, 2001.

8.   Bill Joy, "Technology and Poverty Reduction in the 21st Century, "in Nancy Bearg Dyke (ed.), *The International Poverty Gap: Investing in People & Technology to Build Sustainable Pathways Out* (Washington, D.C.: Aspen Institute, 2000) pp.157-162.

9.   Per Pinstrup-Andersen, Rajul Pandya-Lorch, and Mark Rosengrant, "The World Food Situation: Recent Developments, Emerging Issues, and Long-Term Prospects." In *Food Policy Report* (Washington, DC: International Food Policy Research Institute, 1997).

10.   Gabrielle J. Persley (ed.), *Focus 2: Biotechnology for Developing-Country Agriculture: Problems and Opportunities* (Washington, D.C.: International Food Policy Research Institute, 1999).

11.   Carlos Braga, "The Networking Revolution: Opportunities and Challenges for Developing Countries." infoDev Working Paper (Washington, D.C.: World Bank, 2000).

12.   World Bank, *World Development Report 2000/01: Attacking Poverty* (Washington, D.C.: World Bank, 2000); International Telecommunication Union, *World Telecommunication Development Report 1999* (Geneva: ITU, 1999).

13.   Francisco Rodríguez and Ernest J. Wilson III, "Are Poor Countries Losing the Information Revolution?" infoDev working paper (Washington, D.C.: World Bank, 2000).

14.   EnterpriseSearch is available at <http://www.enterpriseworks.org>.

15.   In December 1997, in Broadway, England, at The Aspen Institute conference, "Persistent Poverty In Developing Countries: Determining the Causes and Closing the Gaps," Jacques Attali presented the case for the creation of a new international institution that would link information technologies and concepts of microfinance to maximize their potential for poverty reduction. Thus, PlaNet Finance was created in November 1998 to support the development of microfinance using the Internet as its primary tool.

16.   See http://www.microcreditsummit.org.

17.   Greenstar, see <http://www.greenstar.org/pressroom/TIME%20Telecenters.htm> and <http://www.greenstar.org/components.htm>.

18.   World Bank, *World Development Report 1998/1999: Knowledge for Development* (New York: Oxford University Press, 1998).

19.   Scott J. Wallsten, *An Empirical Analysis of Competition, Privatization and Regulation in Africa and Latin America* (Stanford Institute for Economic Policy Research, 1999, mimeograph).

20.   A. Izaguirre, *Private Participation in Telecommunications—Recent Trends. Public Policy for the Private Sector Note No. 204* (Washington, D.C.: World Bank, 1999).

21.   Braga, "The Networking Revolution."

22.   Robert Schware, et al., Internet Economic Toolkit for African Policy Makers (Washington, D.C.: World Bank, 1999). Available at <http://www.infodev.org/projects/finafcon.htm>

23.   Organisation for Economic Cooperation and Development, Development Assistance Committee. "Development Cooperation: 2000 Report." DAC Journal 2001 2(1).

24.   Ibid.

25. World Bank, *World Global Development Finance 2001: Building Coalitions for Effective Development Finance* (Washington, D.C.: World Bank, 2001).

26. An up-to-date list of new articles on the topic of HIV/AIDS drug distribution and the plans to establish an international trust fund are available at http://www.cid.harvard.edu/cidinthenews/pr/PCPR040401.html.

27. Robert I. Rotberg, "Africa's Mess, Mugabe's Mayhem." *Foreign Affairs* 79:5, September/October 2000.

28. World Bank, *World Development Report 2000/2001: Attacking Poverty* (Washington, D.C.: World Bank and Oxford University Press, 2000).

29. Iqbal Quadir, "Loud and Near," in *Alleviating Global Poverty: Technology for Economic and Social Uplift,* in Nancy Bearg Dyke (ed.) (Washington, D.C.: Aspen Institute, 2001); Frances Cairncross, *The Death of Distance: How the Communications Revolution Will Change Our Lives* (Cambridge, MA: Harvard Business School, 1997).

30. David Landes, *The Wealth and Poverty of Nations: Why Some Are So Rich and Some So Poor* (New York: W.W. Norton, 1999).

31. Emmanuel Ablo and Ritva Reinikka, "Do Budgets Really Matter?" Policy Research Working Paper 1926 (Washington, D.C.: World Bank, 1998).

32. Wolfgang H. Reinicke and Francis Deng, with Jan Martin Witte, Thorsten Benner, Beth Whitaker, and John Gershman. *Critical Choices: The United Nations, Networks, and the Future of Global Governance* (Ottawa: International Development Research Centre, 2000).

33. International Campaign to Ban Landmines, see <http://www.icbl.org/>.

34. World Commission on Dams, see <http://www.dams.org>.

35. African Development Bank, African Economic Research Consortium, Global Coalition for Africa, United Nations Economic Commission for Africa, and the World Bank, *Can Africa Claim the 21st Century?* (Washington, D.C.: World Bank, 2000).

36. William J. Carrington and Enrica Detragiache, "How Big Is the Brain Drain?" Working Paper 98/102 (Washington, D.C.: International Monetary Fund, 1998).

37. Peter T. Knight, "Lessons from infoDev Education Projects" (Washington, D.C.: Knight-Moore Telematics for Education and Development/CDI, 2000). Available at <http://www.knight-moore.com/pubs/Lessons_from_infoDev_Projects.html>.

38. African Virtual University, see <http://www.avu.org/>.

39. World Bank, *World Development Report 1999/2000: Entering the 21st Century* (Washington, D.C.: World Bank and Oxford University Press, 1999).

40. Nayan Chanda, "Gates and Ghandi." *Far Eastern Economic Review,* 24 August 2000.

41. Higher education was a major topic at the 1999 conference, with a substantial list of recommendations. Nancy Bearg Dyke (ed), *The International Poverty Gap: Investing in People and Technology to Build Sustainable Pathways Out* (Washington, DC: The Aspen Institute, 2000) p.11-13; 61-72.

42. Additional information is available at <http://www.greenstar.org>.

43. The U.S. Library of Congress, "American Memory." Available at <http://memory.loc.gov>. UNESCO, "Memory of the World." Available at <http://www.uncsco.org/webworld/mdm/index_2.html>.

44. Amartya Sen, *Development As Freedom* (New York: Anchor Books, 2000).

INTERNET LINKS

Nongovernmental Organizations and Private Foundations

African Virtual University: http://www.avu.org
Aspen Institute: http://www.aspeninstitute.org
Costa Rica Foundation for Sustainable Development:
       http://www.entebbe.com; http://www.lincos.net
International Campaign to Ban Landmines: http://www.icbl.org
United Nations Foundation: http://www.unfoundation.org
The Youth Employment Summit: http://www.edc/spotlight/YES2001/role.htm

Government Aid Agencies and Multilateral Institutions

Global Development Gateway: http://www.worldbank.org/gateway
G-8: http://www.g7.utoronto.ca
Information for Development (infoDev): http://www.infodev.org
International Telecommunications Union: http://www.itu.int
National Renewable Energy Lab: http://www.nrel.gov/
United Nations: http://www.un.org
United Nations Development Program: http://www.undp.org
United Nations Educational, Scientific and Cultural Organization:
     http://www.unesco.org
World Bank: http://www.worldbank.org
World Health Organization: http://www.who.org
U.S. Agency for International Development: http://www.info.usaid.gov
U.S. Library of Congress, "American Memory": http://memory.loc.gov

Entrepreneurship Programs

Business Partners for Development (BPD): http://www.bpdweb.org/projects.htm
EnterpriseWorks: http://www.enterpriseworks.org
Peoplink: http://peoplink.org

Microfinance Institutions

Grameen Bank: http://www.grameen-info.org
PlaNet Finance: http://www.planetfinance.org

Technology

GrameenPhone: http://www.grameenphone.com
Grameen Telecom: http://grameen-info.org/grameen/gtelecom
Greenstar: http://www.greenstar.org
Infosys Technologies Limited: http://www.inf.com/infosys.htm
Little Intelligent Communities (LINCOS): http://www.lincos.net
The Software Technology Park Scheme: http://www.soft.net
Sun Microsystems: http://www.sun.com
The World Commission on Dams: http://www.dams.org

Speeches

Poverty and Technology: Meeting the Challenge*

By Shashi Tharoor**
August 18, 2000

I'd like to welcome all of you to this third in the series of Aspen Institute conferences on global poverty. I think that everyone will agree with me that the first two conferences were characterized by what we see here: a combination of distinguished participants, first-rate intellectual contributions, lively discussions, and very impressive reports by conference staff. I am also very pleased that we have today, as Conference Chairman, President José María Figueres, whose distinguished record in meeting the challenge of development in his country (Costa Rica) is a great asset for all of us.

The topic before us today is a vital one, and it offers us a new challenge to make a difference here. Are we simply recycling ideas that have been mouthed in endless conferences elsewhere? What can we contribute that is original and useful at the same time?

I think it is helpful to stress early on that we should not worry about hammering out a consensus. This should not be a theoretical exercise in coming up with conclusions about issues in the abstract. In fact, there is a wonderful old story about two professors discussing a practical problem in a symposium rather like this one.

> One of them says, "Do you know how we can solve this?"
> "If we do this and this and this, we can solve it," the other replies.
> And the professor says, "Yes I know, that will work in practice; but will it work in theory?"

And that is precisely the sort of syndrome that we need to avoid. We do not have to worry about the theory of all this. If we can focus on practical applications in discussing the issues before us, we will have accomplished something worthwhile over the next couple of days.

* Presented at the Aspen Institute International Peace, Security & Prosperity Program conference on "Alleviating Global Poverty: Technology for Economic and Social Uplift," August 18-20, 2000.

** Shashi Tharoor was Director of Communications and Special Projects, Office of the Secretary General of the United Nations at the time of the conference. He is now Interim Head, United Nations Department of Information.

There is no doubt that the alleviation of poverty is a realizable goal. United Nations statistics suggest that over the past three decades more than 20 industrialized states and over a dozen developing countries have actually succeeded in eliminating absolute poverty. In order to put our discussion in context, I will share some other UN statistics with you, just to remind us of the scale of the challenge we are facing. There are 1.2 billion people living in absolute poverty. We define this as people living on less than one dollar a day. Keep in mind, there is also double that number of people—2.8 billion, half the world's population—living on less than two dollars a day. There are 750 million unemployed and 750 million underemployed. Another 1.5 billion are without clean drinking water; 800 million have no health services whatsoever, nor access to any; 33 million people suffer from HIV/AIDS. Finally, there are 850 million illiterate people. For all we know, some of these numbers may be undercounts, especially as some of these people now have more children sharing their lot in life. Combating poverty and its effects is truly a gigantic task, which makes these discussions all the more vital and relevant.

It is also appropriate that at this gathering we are going to be focusing on technology. Obviously, technology is on everyone's mind on the cusp of the new millennium, but it is also an issue that can cut both ways, particularly information technology. There is a long list of technologies that can widen the disparities that have brought us around this conference table today. The great risk is that as information technology unveils new models, it may increasingly plunge the poor into more hopelessness and marginalization than ever before. The digital divide has become a catchphrase, one we at the United Nations are conscious of because the vast majority of our members see themselves on the wrong side of the digital divide. And there is no doubt that the present information revolution, like the French Revolution, is a revolution with a lot of *liberté*, some *fraternité*, and no *egalité*. It is a revolution in which there are stark divisions both between countries and within countries.

So when we speak of alleviating poverty in the context of this discussion, we have to think of the very real situation—that the poverty line is not the only line. There is also the high speed digital line, the fiber optic line—all the lines that are known to be transforming the fortunes of many around the world and simultaneously leaving others out. The key lies in the keyboard, and there are a lot of people who do not have access to a keyboard. In fact, my co-moderator at the last conference, Tom Friedman (*New York Times* foreign affairs columnist), loves saying that "the Internet ties us together," and the truth is it does, but who is the "us"? There are still hundreds of millions of people who are not tied to the Internet and therefore cannot be tied to the rest of world through the Internet. I know that people like Jacques Attali (President, PlaNet Finance) and others are working in this area and on other important technology tools we will discuss, and there is much for us to learn from their stories in our discussions today.

I would like now to introduce, with great pleasure, José María Figueres, who is going to be chairman of the conference and our keynote speaker. He has an extraordinary background. In fact, it is particularly striking that at a very young age he has managed different careers and real accomplishments in the private sector, the philanthropic non-profit sector, and the governmental sector. Most notably, when he was elected President of Costa Rica in February of 1994 for the single term that Costa Rican presidents are allowed, he was the youngest president of Costa Rica and also one of the youngest presidents anywhere in the world. He has studied industrial engineering at West Point (the U.S. Military Academy), and he has a Masters in Public Administration from the John F. Kennedy School of Government at Harvard University. It is fascinating that before registering for classes at Harvard he had already been Minister of Foreign Trade and Minister of Agriculture in the Costa Rican government. Earlier, he helped restructure his family business, making it a leading enterprise, particularly in agro-industry. He has chaired and been active in a number of foundations, in particular, The Foundation for Sustainable Development in Costa Rica, which he founded. This foundation is highly relevant to our concerns in this meeting because it supports technological application initiatives to try to enhance the quality of life for people within the framework of sustainability. So, with those brief words of introduction I am very pleased to hand the floor to our chairman, José María Figueres.

Effective Poverty Reduction: Sustainable Development and Information Technology*

Keynote Address by José María Figueres**
August 18, 2000

I would like to start us off this afternoon, if I may, by sharing some dimensions of the poverty alleviation challenge, some of its causes, and some of its possible solutions. I would like to do that within the scope of Latin America. Please forgive my regional scope. I feel more comfortable with the statistics and some of the issues and opportunities in Latin America. And I feel that there are both positive and not-so-positive experiences that can be extrapolated. I would also like to go into some of the applications of technology that can help us to alleviate poverty.

I feel that if we link sustainable development with a new attitude towards development and current information technology, we can really progress in alleviating poverty in new ways. If I can position myself in outer space and watch our planet turn on its axes and ask myself, "Which one of the continents is in a position to take advantage of globalization?," I would have to bet on Latin America. I would have done so because during the last two decades this continent has undergone an enormous amount of impressive transformation—from democratization efforts in political terms, to market economies better positioned between the market and the state, and of course towards respect for human rights. We thought these changes would open up the doors to development and would decrease poverty. Unfortunately and in spite of all this progress, there is one big ugly factor— poverty has increased. In a population of 500 million in Latin America, today we have 200 million poor people. If we have been achieving all these very important transformations on the one hand, and on the other hand, one of the byproducts has been an increase in poverty, this poses a question

*   Speech delivered at the Aspen Institute International Peace, Security & Prosperity Program conference, "Alleviating Global Poverty: Technology for Economic and Social Uplift," in Aspen, Colorado, August 18-20, 2000.

** José María Figueres is former President of Costa Rica; Founder, The Foundation for Sustainable Development; and Managing Director, Center for the Global Agenda, World Economic Forum.

about the style of development we have been leading. That catches my attention.

Not only has poverty increased, but today Latin America is the most unequal region of the world, a double negative point. High levels of inequality reflect an excess of poverty. If inequality in Latin America reflected the same conditions of inequality as in the rest of the world, there would be half the number of poor people in Latin America. We would cut the number of people living in poverty by 100 million. Therefore, this makes my questions about the development style we have been leading even more relevant and urgent. If we assumed an average 2% GNP growth, which is not very much, inequality levels would remain constant. We already have enough evidence to show that the inequality and the levels of poverty in Latin America are, in and of themselves, obstacles to greater economic growth. Hence, we are in a dilemma that is going to be difficult to escape.

Let us focus on Central America, a region that most suffered the effects of the Cold War during the last 50 years. With the help of some of you around this table, Central America has really come through a peace process. It is moving towards the scripting of democracies, which we know is much more than holding elections every four years, and towards an integration of Central America as a competitor in the global economy. Do we want Central America to compete on the old basis of competitiveness, degradation of natural resources and low salaries? Or, do we want to shift the paradigm of competitiveness towards value-added productivity, technology, and efficiency so we can then begin to address some of the underlying social problems? I make the argument that the latter is the option we want.

And, of course, as in the case of Latin America, in spite of the important and very beneficial changes that we have seen in Central America, poverty alleviation is also a major challenge. Poverty is measured by rural and urban population; and we can see cases where the average of poor people in populated and rural areas is probably around 80% of the population and in urban areas around 50%. The situation has transpired despite all the changes that we have gone through in the course of development. Therefore, questions challenging the style of development we have been leading are all the more important.

Now, I would like to share some of the different factors affecting poverty and the way we look at them in Latin America. I would like to group these together in four categories: political, economic, social, and environmental. First, on the political front, poor quality of governance, corruption, and inefficiency are the major factors contributing to poverty. A sincere lack of responsible and sensitive political leadership also impedes attempts at poverty reduction. Poverty is not an issue that is tackled in a holistic and serious way. We certainly give it a lot of lip service, but we are not committing our minds, our thoughts, our spirits, and our resources to a high quality of poverty alleviation. Weak commitments and political goals are the outcome of this lack of resolve to combat poverty. Of course, the lack of participation channels in political processes for those who are poor only mirrors the fact that they are excluded from the market. The market perceives signals from consumers. The poor do not consume; and so therefore, they fall under the radar screen of the market. The poor are under the radar screen of the market and without channels of accessibility to the political decision-making processes. What a tremendous dilemma.

Second, the insufficient economic growth adversely affects the goal of poverty reduction. We need to grow between 5% and 7% per year. We have already discussed some of the reasons why we cannot achieve that; but to compound those challenges, we are still very vulnerable to the rest of the world's economy. Whatever occurs negatively in the world's economy has an impact on Latin America. The benefits of economic growth are not auto matic. To those who believe in the trickledown theory, there is no trickledown. It never gets to where it is supposed to get. There is a narrow applicability of economic policies, meaning there are no good sound economic policies to combat poverty. We have economic policies for good macroeconomic balances and for many other issues, but we lack those to combat poverty.

Third, in terms of social factors—poor health conditions are a critical problem. If we do not have good health, how can we be productive? There has been a complete recasting of what we mean by good health. Good health is no longer large hospitals as we have previously thought of it in many parts of the world. Good health should begin with preventive medicine programs. We are lacking a commitment to those in the region and perhaps in the world. Additionally, a lack of educational opportunities impedes the alleviation of poverty. I cannot say enough about the need to revolutionize our education experience. This system of public schools has its origins in the Industrial Revolution. Children who come to kindergarten are as creative as our scientists. Then we began to layer off their creativity and teach them to be a product for the Industrial Revolution—get a job, 8 to 5, do it the same way every day, do it all their life. In the new Technology Revolution we need to change so that we learn to learn instead of learning to know something. And, deteriorating housing conditions also have a clear impact on alleviation of poverty because there is a complete sociological dimension to home conditions.

Finally, environmental factors have clear impact on poverty alleviation. Our next conference should be called "*Alleviating Global Poverty: Technology for Economical, Social and Environmental Uplift.*" The environment has a lot to do with poverty issues in our part of the world—and I would say the globe over—as a result of irrational depletion of natural resources and natural disasters associated with environmental mismanagement, such as El Niño, La Niña, and Hurricane Mitch. The Aspen Institute is celebrating its fiftieth anniversary—unfortunately, progress in Nicaragua has just been pushed back 50 years with Hurricane Mitch. They are going to have an even harder time getting out of poverty conditions as a direct result of Mitch. It is very difficult to begin to construct growth based on our natural resources in a responsible way.

With these different factors, lumped in four categories, it is obvious that we need a holistic approach to alleviating poverty. There is no easy solution and I would propose that we need some good actors in this cause against poverty—and we also need a winning strategy to outline what those actors should do. Let's begin with two of our actors—the market and the government. This relates to one of the assumptions given to us for this conference and which came out of the October 1999 Aspen Institute poverty conference—the market can do a lot to alleviate poverty. In this context, macroeconomic stability and a friendly environment for international trade and foreign investment mean we have to bring them packaged together in order to move forward the political agenda.

However, we in the developing countries bear the primary responsibility for helping to create the necessary conditions so we can begin to eliminate poverty. That raises a second very important factor that we have often shunned in recent times because we say the state is big, inefficient, loud, noisy, and does not deliver with a bang—the strategic role of the state. Government positions do matter. And we need to reinforce the importance of having good institutions that commit themselves to their missions and push them forward—good governance, institutional efficiency, and priority set on social sector investments, especially education and health. Our goal is to protect the poorest of the poor. We do need the sound governance, institutional efficiency, and strong priorities; and the institutions do need a helping hand.

At the same time we should remember the concept of empowerment. If we get the actors together and abandon this Cold War philosophy of having the private sector on one hand and the government of the other, then it seems we need a new strategy. There may be several options, but I would also make the case for shifting the paradigm of development from the way we have known it in the past towards sustainable development. When one looks again at all the reforms that have gone into Latin America while at the same time problems have increased, one has to come to the conclusion that we are not doing something right in the equation of development. If we focus on sustainable development, achieve our macrobalances, increase internal saving and external rates of investment, and at the same time and with equal emphasis put forward a strategic program of investment in human development and declare or construct an alliance with nature, we will do a lot more in terms of extracting value from globalization and taking it to those people that need this value the most.

Let me now leave discussion of a theoretical framework and go to a specific example. I will use the example of Costa Rica. While shifting the paradigm towards sustainable development in Costa Rica, we very rapidly came to the conclusion that when we began to combine these three cornerstones of macroeconomic stability, strategic human development investments, and an alliance with nature, we really maximized their value. And of course we also would be able to achieve that if we were able to integrate the networks of services that are available to combat poverty—networks of health services, education, and technology information infrastructure. We will look at these in a little detail. For example, instead of having distinct hospitals and clinics, which are the least common denominator of our preventive health policy, we integrated them together to work as a system, which had never been done in the past. Or, for example, instead of wasting the very limited resources in our university systems allotted for research and investigation, we began to coordinate it through a high technology national center. Even the network of micro-optics, in a country with 52,000 kilometers had to lay out 10,000 kilometers of optic fiber. In one way we are beginning to build the backbone and in another we are continuing to build and construct the last mile. Our parks, which are 30% of our national territory, are no longer parks on an individual basis, but instead are a network. Making all this happen and work as a network in order to create better nets to combat poverty and push development issues is not easy, but I would argue that we are making some progress. It is not easy because of balancing the short-term immediate demands versus the medium and longer scope of sustainability in our development is always something that is very hard to blend together.

On top of that we had to construct what we would call the information society, meaning a society that wants information to travel to where the people are and not the people to have to travel to where the information is. A second and very important part of the definition is that we want this to be a democratic exercise. This is not an activity for the 20% at the top of the economic ladder; this is an activity for the people at the bottom. There are many applications today of information technology that can reinforce the three corners of sustainable development.

For example, in terms of health, telemedicine projects link hospitals or clinics with doctors in other areas of the country and enable them to examine patients in other areas of the country. Without the technology, they would have to travel, which might not be possible. In the case of our educational network, 100% of high schools with computers have the potential to give every one of 350,000 high school students in Costa Rica an e-mail address by the end of next year. If every family had access to the Internet, it could create the synergies and the possibilities of an information society.

In the financial area, the use of Smart Cards means that the progressive use of technology is aimed at reducing poverty levels. We have a smart card program in a rural area and have issued 57,000 smart cards with a total published of 65,000. With this you are beginning to bring the informal sector, which is so linked with poverty, into the formal sector. These smart cards can be used, as they are in Costa Rica, to pay for the bus service and the public phone and to begin to create many different diverse circumstances in which technology is aiding development.

In terms of our environmental programs, with technology we can more accurately monitor our carbon monoxide levels. In 1995, we passed a fossil fuel tax that is really an emission tax in the forestry law. It provided us with a forestry department that purchases environmental services. The money gets reinvested in the hydrological basis of the project. This has allowed Costa Rica to establish a second greenhouse gas law, which is placing Certifiable Tradable Offsets (CTOs) outside of Costa Rica. These certifiable tradable carbon offsets certified by SGS in Switzerland are attracting, together with our potential in this field, up to an additional 2.3% of GNP in the way of payment for environmental services.

Does all this pay off? Well, it is a lot of hard work; and yes, it does pay off. Costa Rica grew 8% in 1998, 7% in 1999, and we are going to grow another 7% again this year. Foreign investment is up at a level never experienced. Additionally, we are beginning to see the putting together of a new type of society and the alleviation of some of the endemic problems we have always faced in our country.

Now, what else can we do, because there are still many other things to be done. In recent years I have been associated with a small foundation in Costa Rica, The Foundation for Sustainable Development, which promotes the application of information technology. LINCOS, which stands for its acronym in English, Little Intelligent Communities, is such an effort. LINCOS promotes people and their well being through the application of cost effective and efficient technologies within the framework of sustainable development. It is a collaborative effort between universities, the private sector and communities. The structure of a LINCOS unit is a funny-looking container that has outlived its use as a transportation mode. We completely refurbish the unit adding a computer lab for educational facilities and telediagnostic and telemedicine possibility. The community can build a small entrepreneurial public phone system or voice over the Internet program around video conferencing. These are merely some of the opportunities we offer through the LINCOS unit. A LINCOS unit is set up under a tent to cover it and provide cover for the amphitheater that is built around it. In San Marcos De Tarrazu, a very poor rural community, people are now growing aquatic horticulture with information they found on the web. There is a coffee farmer who is getting three times what he used to get for his coffee production because he set up an elementary web page. There are all types of exciting and innovative experiences that begin to arise when people have access to community-run technology and service. Another example of the impact of a LINCOS unit is in the Dominican Republic. There was no phone access in a secluded rural village, and now all of a sudden, using the LINCOS unit, they communicate through e-mail with their relatives who work in the United States.

Where is this LINCOS initiative going? It has four components. We hope to have employed 35-40 LINCOS units in the Central America area by the end of next year. The second component is a monitoring facility that will record and register what the communities are using in the LINCOS units and what they are not. Additionally, the monitor will determine what the communities look at as possible needs they have that should be supplied by the LINCOS unit, so that we can begin to create software for people in rural areas. This will remedy the fact that so far they have been off the market screen. The third component is a LINCOS lab. This takes the information generated in the monitoring center and begins to translate it into practical solutions, which then are implemented in the containers that have been deployed. And the fourth concept is the importance of learning as a community around the LINCOS unit. We want this to become the community center of the 21st century. Around these many different possibilities we will create the conditions that really empower people in rural areas. All of this goes towards our standing commitment to reduce poverty while increasing the opportunities of well-being, linking education and technology in a way in which we really transform communities. By moving beyond education in the classical way we have known it so far, we allow these small communities in rural communities to become a world-class competitive platform no longer divided from the rest of the world by the geographical areas of the maps.

Technology and Poverty*

By Bill Joy**
August 18, 2000

In my work I normally deal with a 10-year planning horizon. But since we are at the celebration of the 50th anniversary of The Aspen Institute, I would like to look out a little farther to how technology will affect global poverty over the next fifty years. In this timeframe, we will go well beyond the current second wave of globalization and beyond the ongoing transformation to an information society.

We can easily imagine that the changes that are going to occur in the next fifty years will be on the scale of the change of the industrial revolutions, which played out in a couple of phases over quite a long period. This time, the changes will play out much more quickly.

In the 21st century, science and technology will give us the tools to achieve mastery over the physical world, to the limits of physical law. With genetic engineering and proteomics we are likely to be able to cure many diseases and greatly extend people's life spans. Explosive new technology like nanotechnology and robotics should make most material goods incredibly inexpensive. Robotics is also likely to greatly limit the need for grinding physical labor. These new technologies will create an enormous amount of new wealth, perhaps 1,000 trillion US dollars. With such new wealth available, we will have the opportunity to easily eliminate material poverty, if we so choose.

A specific set of new 21st century technologies that I call GNR—genetics, nanotechnology, and robotics—is information technologies. You will be able to play with them on your personal computer, so you can design—for good or for evil—without the need for a large laboratory. Soon, for example, biology will be driven by information-based techniques—genomics and proteomics—as we saw with Celera Genomics sequencing the human genome using robots and computers. We saw the kids in the Philippines and

* Presented at the Aspen Institute International Peace, Security & Prosperity Program conference, "Alleviating Global Poverty: Technology for Economic and Social Uplift," August 18-20, 2000.

** Bill Joy is Co-Founder and Chief Scientist, Sun Microsystems, Inc.

in Montreal shutting down the Internet with just software. Worse things can happen in the physical world through abuses of GNR technologies.

Information-based technologies benefit large organizations, but can also be abused by people on a newly small scale. Industrial and information technologies historically have had the effect of centralizing power, as it did in the industrial revolution. The Internet certainly accelerates this effect, making large companies more successful. But the GNR technologies are dematerializing in such a way that enables people with bad intent to do things in a way that provides a counterpoint to the historic centralization of power. Thus, information technology simultaneously both centralizes and decentralizes power.

The history of industrialization is replete with initial horrors. Industrialization brought grinding child labor, destruction of the family, massive pollution, and destructive political movements that took more than a century to overcome. The major bad consequences of information technology that we are likely to have to mitigate are the corrosion of local cultures due to communications technologies and the rise in terrorism using information technologies and GNR. It is in our clear self-interest to work to sensibly mitigate these negative effects.

I am optimistic that the new technologies will soon create enough material goods that we can choose to eliminate poverty and give everyone basic health care. But, that alone is not sufficient—in a post-scarcity world we must also help people find meaning in their lives. Finding this meaning will be the greatest challenge to our global capitalist civilization in this new century.

Discussion Papers

and

Prepared Remarks

Loud and Near*

By Iqbal Z. Quadir**

ABSTRACT

Digital technologies will help alleviate poverty around the world by improving governance, the poor quality of which has perpetuated poverty. People—including the very poor—can help themselves if they live in an enabling environment, which is governed by the rule of law and provides opportunities to apply their energies and skills.

This paper argues that governance cannot be improved through a top-down process, and further, that the top-down development approach may have contributed to worsening governance. However, declining costs and increasing utility are helping digital technologies spread rapidly even in poor countries with or without top-down initiatives, potentially improving the environment in which the poor live and work.

While in concept governments solve collective problems, how far governments will actually go in carrying out their responsibilities depends on what people are able to demand from their governments.[1] Quality of governance naturally depends on the extent to which the authorities listen to people. As a result, it boils down to how loudly or assertively people are able to speak and how near they are to the authorities.

The spread of digital tools can improve the distribution of economic clout, and therefore increase the number of people with a political voice. In addition, widely available information and new forms of connectivity are leading to devolution of authority, thereby bringing authorities nearer to peoples.

IMPROVING GOVERNANCE IS KEY TO ALLEVIATING POVERTY.

According to a recent *New York Times* article, "From a village-eye view where life is harshest, some development experts say, nothing could be more irrelevant than global theories or rants against multinational companies. To the poorest people who live without teachers, doctors, roads, electricity, and sometimes even food and water, the culprit is a lot closer to home: the local, state or national government."[2] The article quotes Kofi Annan, the United Nations Secretary General, that "the issue is primarily that of governance—how the international community of sovereign states

* Paper commissioned for the Aspen Institute International Peace, Security & Prosperity Program conference "Alleviating Global Poverty: Technology for Economic and Social Uplift," August 18-20, 2000.

** Iqbal Quadir is Co-Founder of GrameenPhone in Bangladesh.

and multilateral organizations cope with global challenges, and how individual nations manage their own affairs so as to play their part, pull their weight and serve their peoples."[3]

While the world expects governments to "serve their peoples," "nearly 100 armed conflicts since the end of the Cold War have virtually all been intrastate affairs...with governments acting against their own citizens, through extreme corruption, violence, incompetence, or complete breakdown..."[4] In relatively more peaceful places, the vast masses of small business owners operate between a rock and a hard place. Millions of small businesses operate in the daunting extralegal (informal) environment not to avoid taxes—as such an environment is very taxing due to limitations on investment, credit and scale of operation, and extortion by local bullies—but because they find the legal (formal) environment inhospitable.[5] The legal environment is challenging even for very determined entrepreneurs. In 1981, Narayana Murthy founded Infosys Technologies in India, a company with current market capitalization of US $16 billion. It took 18 months for Murthy to get the necessary licenses from his democratically elected government.[6] Governments do attempt to stamp out corruption and to make bureaucracies people-friendly. However, their efforts are impeded by natural barriers when they use bureaucracies to solve problems with roots in the very nature of bureaucracy. In China, where communist party officials are known to sell government posts for personal gain, one enterprising official even sold the post of the chief of the anticorruption bureau for US$31,300.[7]

While in theory economic progress "requires an effective state, one that plays a catalytic, facilitating role, encouraging and complementing the activities of private business and individuals,"[8] in reality, people actually spend a considerable amount of energy protecting themselves against predatory state machinery. Imagine how many successful entrepreneurs in Silicon Valley would have given up if they encountered the same difficulties that Narayana Murthy did in India. Imagine again how much poorer America would be as a result. It is not just the frustration the entrepreneurs undergo, but the progress the country forgoes.

The problems of governance, of course, go beyond the operation of the state machinery, and into the area of policies, which are not necessarily directed to the well being of people. Building infrastructure exclusively in the urban areas, while neglecting rural communities as governments typically do in poor countries, leads to rural-to-urban migration and pushes urban land prices to the stratosphere, while land prices in the rural areas decline. This not only favors the urban rich at the expense of the rural poor, worsening income and wealth distributions, it also raises the cost of doing business. Businesses either crowd to the urban areas, where land prices and rents are extremely high, or suffer through the absence of infrastructure in the rural areas. Trade barriers that typically protect a handful of domestic manufacturers do so at the expense of a large number of consumers. The premium prices commanded by protected manufacturers shift potential economic surplus from the masses to a handful of merchants. The generous packages (for example, tax incentives and favorable deals in privatization projects) governments offer to foreign companies to attract investments are typically a compensation for poor governance, the poor governance that led to an unattractive investment climate in the first place.

The problem of governance is, of course, as old as governments. At the beginning of the last millennium, China was the most advanced society in the world. "What led the greatly advanced civilization of China to fall behind Europe was its government clamping down too tightly as to leave no room for new development."[9]

While the governance problem is somewhat recognized, people in today's prosperous countries tend to take good governance for granted. They assume that governments in all places play a responsible role, as they probably see in their own prosperous countries. The presentation of a recent article by *The Economist* with regard to ways countries can benefit from information technologies (IT) included the following in its concluding section, right after a section dedicated to developing countries.

> Governments retain an important role in ensuring that the opportunities offered by IT are fully exploited. Well-functioning markets for labor, products and capital are important, but on their own they are not enough. Investment in education, too, will be crucial, to ensure that the workforce is equipped for the information economy. America, in particular, needs to get moving on that.[10]

Being mindful of the usual free-market tilt of *The Economist*, one could probably gather that most people probably place an even higher degree of confidence in governments, and their ability to solve problems. If governments were so prudent or so capable, then poverty would have already ceased to exist; there are plenty of examples of good government policies that have alleviated poverty. In the past, in many poor countries, governments far from ensured that their citizens fully exploit opportunities offered by technologies. What makes us think they will this time? Well-functioning markets for labor, products, and capital are apparently not enough, but do even these basic market conditions exist in poor countries? Investment in education needs to be made. Did we not need this investment in education in the "old economy?" What did governments do then? If governments had failed earlier, what will make them succeed now? Interestingly enough, *The Economist* suggests that America, where most of the information revolution is taking place at the moment, needs to make more investment in education. If America—the country with the most democratic, transparent, and resourceful government in the world—is being told in what direction it should move, does that not indicate how difficult it is to mobilize governments in general?

The assumption of congruence between the state and the nation misleads us in our understanding of the problems in poor countries. In many cases, the nation-state, the main political unit with which the world community is built, is a problematic concept. In reality, the state is often in conflict with the nation. Real progress will be made if poor countries succeed in bringing the state into harmony with the nation, a harmony that cannot be taken for granted.

IN REALITY, COUNTRIES ARE GOVERNED BY VESTED INTERESTS.

While some of Karl Marx's economic reasoning may have been wrong, he did have a powerful economic insight in the 1840s while working as a journalist that drove him to study economics. Marx was "convinced of the economic basis of politics—that underlying political theories and political power lay the economic interests of various groups in society."[11] Thus, the quality of governance is dependent on the distribution of economic clout, because it is only people with sufficient economic clout that are able to speak loudly enough for governments to hear. This may explain why poor countries' policies are biased towards urban rich, favoring infrastructure in the urban areas, protection of local manufacturers, and minimal, if any, provisions to empower the poor. To governments in poor countries, the urban rich are loud and near, others silent and distant.

This vested interests theory also explains why policy makers do not necessarily adopt good policies even if they know ways to alleviate poverty. Had politicians and policy makers set out to eliminate poverty, poverty and misery would already have been eliminated. Poverty exists in countries because their governments have gotten away with not implementing the requisite healthy policies—the poor were simply not able to exert enough political pressure. There is extensive literature on how a country can make political and economic progress.[12] The fact that such advice is not followed and poverty continues to exist for nearly half the world's population only confirms the rule of vested interests.

The telecommunications sector can provide a non-abstract example that wisdom alone is not adequate—governments do not necessarily follow established wisdom if vested interests dictate a different opinion. Research done by the International Telecommunication Union (ITU) has established that each new telephone in a poor country boosts that country's annual Gross National Product (GNP) by a factor of three-to-four times the one-time cost of installing the line. At the same time, the cost of providing telecommunications services is decreasing with the prices of microchips.

Moreover, the telecommunications infrastructures, if in place, can act as the backbone of any potential e-economy in these countries. Yet, in most poor countries, people are desperate for telephones and willing to pay more than the tariff in rich countries. If telecommunications means economic growth, as ITU research indicates, then suppression of demand by artificially high prices is suppression of progress. Government-owned telephone companies (who are members of ITU) are often reluctant to reduce tariffs, despite evidence that increased use would compensate for any reduction in revenues due to reduced tariffs. In other words, government-owned companies behave like monopolies by restricting the supply of a service that could act as a vehicle for economic growth.

According to textbooks, capital, technology, and human skills make a country move forward. In the telecommunications example, these are not the issues. The equipment for these networks is fairly standard and available for anyone to purchase. Foreign telecommunications companies are quite willing to set up telephone networks in poor countries with their own expertise and capital, if local governments simply provide adequate permissions (such as licenses) and satisfactory legal frameworks. Thus, lack of telecommunications services in poor countries and its consequent progress are not due to a lack of capital, labor, know-how, or technology, but rather to a lack of political readiness. In fact, if political readiness were obtained, economic progress would follow and capital, labor, know-how, and technology—the ingredients recommended by textbooks for economic progress—would emerge from domestic sources or flow in from abroad.

One could expect counterexamples in communist regimes liberalizing their policies (China in the late 1970s and Russia in the late 1980s) as proof that governments do acquire wisdom on their own to change for the better. However, in these two cases, the vested interests lay in ensuring the survival of the communist parties. Since the parties controlled everything, including the economies that were collapsing due to fundamental flaws of communism, the vested interests required a change in direction.

One could also argue that the governments in East Asian economies, particularly after World War II, somehow had the wisdom to pursue open trade and other liberal policies that dramatically boosted their economies and significantly reduced the proportion of their populations in poverty. Here too, one should note that business interests developed through trade, as American markets were open to these countries due to certain political and military events (American involvement in World War II, Korean War, communist threat, and protection of Taiwan). These business interests developed symbiotic relationships with the governments and drove government policies.[13] The governments, again, pursued goals dictated by vested interests. In these instances, the vested economic interests were consistent with economic growth, investment in plants and equipment, and investment in education. Indeed, such symbiosis between politics and economics built the nation of England. For instance, it was the merchants whose prosperity benefited from the protection of the monarchs and who, in turn, strengthened the monarchs against feudal lords, as seen in the following quote:

> Merchants benefited from the widened trade made possible by a unified economy in which local barriers to commerce were reduced. In turn, the merchants augmented the monarch's power by helping finance the armies needed to subordinate the nobility ...profits [from merchants' trades] would flow to the homeland and domestic manufacturers would be stimulated by the export market. The state gained from the tariff revenues derived from large trade, from the sale of trade monopolies, from the development of strategic military industries and personnel—shipbuilding and ship supplies, sailors and captains—and from the general economic growth that provided a firm base for national power. Two of the basic goals of national policy, therefore, were the development of commerce and its counterparts, the growth of power in international affairs.[14]

In contrast, the vested interests worked differently in India. Business houses that became rich by selling simple products in large domestic markets had no incentive to seek additional markets abroad. They sided with the government's philosophy of self-reliance consistent with the post-colonial sentiment, thus making India an inward-looking non-trading country for nearly five decades. The low growth or stagnation that followed worsened through vested interests working against the larger and poorer segment of its population. The state of Bihar, for instance, which seemed to be in better shape than many others, by many measures, is the worst state socially and economically in India today, illustrating, only more dramatically, what happened in that country.

> At the time of India's independence in 1947, [Bihar's] future looked exceptionally bright. It had abundant resources—rich agricultural land along the Ganges and valuable mineral deposits in the southern mountains—and it also had one of the new country's most competent civil administrations. Unfortunately, though, Bihar's society remained essentially feudal in structure: its principal economic and social relationships ran vertically between the rich and the poor. Most of Bihar's land was owned and controlled by powerful landowning castes, and groups with little or no land were almost entirely dependent on these landowners for their livelihood.[15]

THE KEY TO IMPROVING GOVERNANCE IS INVOLVING THE CITIZENRY.

While governance in reality is determined by vested interests, the citizenry is the best resource to create good governance. Even Niccolo Machiavelli, the old master of power politics and no sentimental admirer of anything including people, wrote nearly 500 years ago that people are a source of sound judgment.

> If we consider princes restricted by laws and people bound by laws, we will find greater

qualities in people than in princes. If we consider them both when unrestrained by laws, we will find people making fewer and less weighty errors than princes, and possessing weightier remedies for them. A corrupt and disorderly multitude can be spoken to by some worthy person and can easily be brought around to the right way, but a bad prince cannot be spoken to by anyone, and the only remedy in his case is cold steel. From this we may conjecture as to which is susceptible to the graver illness; for if words are enough to cure the people's illness and only steel will cure that of a prince, no one will fail to conclude a graver cure argues a graver defect.[16]

Many philosophers and political scientists have discussed the beauties of democracy and the wisdom of common man, which is beyond the scope of this paper. Here, we merely try to emphasize that involving the so-called "low-level" people or ordinary citizens—people who directly experience problems—is the crucial part of solving the problems. A wide range of situations (factory floors, national politics, grass-root development projects, innovations and others) bear this out.

Until recently, the manufacturing process in America was typically structured around "infallible" commands filtered down from the upper echelon of the company. Fredrick Taylor, the founder of management science, argued that "all possible brain work should be removed from the [factory] shop... [workers] are not supposed to think...There are other people paid for thinking around here."[17] In contrast, Japanese factory workers were actively encouraged to provide feedback, following the advice of American statistician W. Edwards Deming. After all, turning off the brains at the factory floor is a massive waste. As it turns out, the Japanese manufacturing plants typically outperformed American ones. In recent years, the feedback techniques—utilizing the wisdom from the bottom—have increasingly been adopted in American plants with positive results.

To the extent apples and oranges can indeed be compared by their constituent parts, the Soviet Union illustrates the effect of wasting the wisdom of common people on a much larger scale. The Soviet Union, motivated by control rather than efficiency, treated the entire nation like Taylor's factory floor, with obvious and more extreme results. Though arguably very different situations, the less than optimal outcome in the American factory floors and the disastrous outcome in the much larger Soviet economy have one thing in common: both ignored the feedback from people who experience the actual problems.[18]

In contrast, it is the increased incorporation of the wishes and opinions of people from "lower levels" that has been at the root of good governance. The rule of law, freedom of speech, and political liberty (which together constitute good governance) began to evolve initially in Western Europe, particularly in England, in the period during and after the Middle Ages. Unlike the past empires of China or India, one of Europe's secrets was the ascendance of its ordinary citizens, and the consequent input they were able to provide in political decision-making.

> The economic expansion of medieval Europe was thus promoted by a succession of organizational innovations and adaptations, most of them initiated from below and diffused by example... *Almost all of this "commercial revolution" came from the mercantile community, bypassing where necessary the rules of this or that city or state,* inventing or improving the new venues for encounter and exchange (ports and outports, faubourgs, local markets, international fairs), creating in short a world of its own like an overlay on the convoluted, inconvenient mosaic of political units [the italics are mine].[19]

Consistent with these experiences, the top-down model of economic development has produced a disproportionate number of failures. After all, the "state-led models of development that came crashing down in the 1980s,"[20] were fundamentally inconsistent with this history of economic progress, not to mention the empirical and theoretical findings of Adam Smith that trade and free enterprise—not state-led economies—produce wealth. Indeed, according to the World Bank, the largest and the most powerful of the institutions involved in the top-down approach, income inequality has widened in the last 40 years, a period when the top-down approach has been pursued most vigorously. "In 1960, per capita GDP [Gross Domestic Product] in the richest 20 countries was 18 times that in the poorest 20 countries. By 1995, this gap has widened to 37 times".[21]

In contrast, one of the most widely recognized successful development models is that of Grameen Bank in Bangladesh, which has started a worldwide micro-credit movement. Where did this innovation originate? From the absolute bottom. The Bank's founder Muhammad Yunus observed that, "Projects imposed on villagers failed to have desired impact; however, when villagers determined the structures and rules, their local organizations had flourished. The lesson? Ask, don't tell... So Yunus assembled the groups of villagers and asked how the loans should be administered. From one of these discussions emerged the decision to form groups to facilitate collection."[22] Thus emerged a revolutionary banking system not requiring collateral, a major departure since the establishment of modern banking in the Italian Renaissance and a change that has benefited millions of poor people around the world. Rather than being an "expert" at the top, the genius of Yunus was his respect for the destitute and his courage in asking them what innovation they needed.

Experts often fail for the simple reason that they rarely themselves experience the problems they attempt to solve. Decision-makers sitting at the top of hierarchies depend on abstract information, but "attending too closely to information overlooks the social context that helps people understand what that information might mean and why it matters."[23] Human decision-making unavoidably uses emotive processes. Relying purely on abstract information or models is actually a loss, not an improvement because it does not take advantage of all our faculties involved in perception.[24] Furthermore, the top-down approach also causes large-scale damage as the top's influence is typically over a large area. In contrast, innovations at the bottom are copied or scaled up only when their merits are proven.

By ignoring the eyes and ears of people who directly experience problems, top-down problem solvers sometime unnecessarily face overwhelming complexity. Democracy and market repeatedly prove themselves to be superior to top-down control or management because democracy and market do not even attempt what is impossible. Instead of accumulating information to a central place and then attempting to find the best solution—straining the central solver to an impossible point—democracy and market attempt to solve problems on a decentralized basis. Kremlin leaders, for instance, took on an impossible job of trying to micromanage a large economy; it was their ability to hide things that made the Soviet system appear smoother than it was. Even a simple and smoothly functioning market would become too complex if one attempted to manage it. Today's Internet is impossible to "manage" from a central control. Like market mechanisms, solutions to complex problems often lie in finding and implementing simple rules whereby a large number of decentralized entities manage themselves. When experts find "complexity, number, and frequency of choices …[growing] beyond the ability to know and decide…[and] skills development in concept formulation and communications decreasing relative to the requirements of an increasingly complicated world,"[25] it may be an indication that we are not utilizing the eyes and ears of people affected by the problems, and not necessarily that the problems are getting too complicated.

Perhaps we should remind ourselves of what Adam Smith, the founder of modern economics, said more than two centuries ago: "In civilized society [man] stands at all times in need of cooperation and assistance of great multitudes".[26] Citizens do not just need good governance and good problem solving. Citizens are the means.

POVERTY LEADS TO SILENCE AND INCREASED STATE POWER LEADS TO LONGER DISTANCE.

While the capacity to solve problems lies in people, poor countries end up with poor solutions to their problems because people are silent and distant. They are disengaged from governance. Vested interests work against peoples' interests and disconnect them from governance, wasting the very resource that would potentially improve it.

While each country has its own complex and unique history, in general the 20th century witnessed a massive rise of both state power[27] and subjugation of individual initiative, even outside the extreme examples of communist and fascist regimes. Different sets of forces operated in rich and poor countries, both coalescing around a top-down development model for poor countries. The effect, however unintentional, was to increase the power of states relative to that of the peoples.

In the last 50 years, in poor countries, local elites found it relatively easy to use the colonial machinery they inherited to extend state power. People in these countries, newly freed from colonialism, put their trust in local leaders and, in the process, may have left more than their due amount of power in the states and in the hands of these leaders. Nationalistic feelings overrode economic priorities and incorporation of proper checks and balances. The existing inequality between the rich and the poor in these countries made it easy for vested economic interests to assert themselves on the state machinery. Furthermore, states gathered enormous power by aligning themselves with one or the other side of the East-West conflict.

On the other hand, for several reasons, in rich countries command-and-control or top-down management became fashionable, particularly after World War II. The victory in the war left a positive impression of the military approach to solving problems. Rich countries were also enjoying economic success through command-and-control corporate structures. "Leaders skilled at control became the leaders of modernity: GM's Alfred Sloan, the United Mine Workers' John L. Lewis, the Pentagon's Robert McNamara, ITT's Harold Geneen."[28] New mathematical tools in operations research, control theory and macroeconomics were extending managers' ability to solve problems involving larger areas, albeit for simplistic problems. This emerging top-down mentality coincided with successful roles played by states—mostly in places where good governance had already emerged—particularly in the economic recoveries from depressions and WWII. In relatively more advanced countries, states also started to play meaningful roles in remedying market externalities (e.g. regulating pollution). In addition, rich (leading) countries were naturally interested in maintaining their spheres of influence as the Cold War deepened. These combined to a clear endorsement, from all sides, of state-led top-down management of economies in many poor countries.

Thus, rich countries, motivated by both good intentions to alleviate poverty and a desire to maintain order, established multilateral organizations that typically sent aid to state machinery in poor countries, reducing the governments' need to listen to the people's voices. "...many of the poorest and least effective states have been 'externally-oriented'...[meaning] that the governing elites have much more incentive to please external agents (other states, large transnational companies) than to build or maintain legitimacy among their own citizens."[29] The voice of people remained faint and far. Not loud and not near.

The fact that aid has a high correlation to political purpose[30] only confirms the role of vested interests. Aid, however, also was justified by academics that claimed that transfer of savings (i.e. capital) would lead to prosperity in poor countries.[31] Such academic models did not, for instance, take into account governance issues that would have been a crucial deciding factor for ordinary investors before making an investment. In other words, policies were made by vested interests, while abstract models provided the rationale. Perhaps to explain that vested interests do indeed rule, John Maynard Keynes had said, "Madmen in authority, who hear voices in the air, are distilling their frenzy from some academic scribbler of a few years back."

When governments in poor countries become "externally oriented," governance deteriorates in three ways, and, more importantly, the external attempts usually fail to reform the system. First, the increased irrelevance of people to outward-looking authority sets off a vicious cycle of unaccountability and poor resolutions of problems. Second, governments in poor countries escape natural forces of reforms by latching onto external sources of power, reform efforts that would naturally arise from within, especially since the miseries of poor countries are somewhat attributable to local problems and local history. Third, a new set of vested interests emerges both in rich and poor countries that live on the aid flow and resist change. The providers of aid have, of course, attempted to reform the system by, for instance, directing aid to specific target sectors and imposing conditions of reforms in exchange for aid. David Dollar, Research Manager of the World Bank Development Research Group, characterizes the effectiveness of these approaches as "myths."[32]

TECHNOLOGICAL INNOVATIONS RECONFIGURE VESTED INTERESTS.

Technological innovations, if their benefits flow to people, shake up vested interests. Among other things, innovations help new classes of entrepreneurs emerge to enlarge the circle of influential people. Moreover, technological innovations usually expand the economic pie while being established, potentially avoiding head-on confrontation with vested interests. In addition to these general effects from technological innovations, digital technologies, in particular, empower ordinary citizens economically and politically, and consequently have an additional impact on reconfiguring vested interests.

Historically, innovations have allowed new players to gain strength, who later became economically and politically influential. Today's "disruptive technologies"—those that fundamentally alter ways of doing business—are not a new phenomenon. Technologies have been disrupting for a long time, and "disruptions" and "reconfigurations" are more descriptive of the phenomenon than "replacement." The Marxist thesis that "The feudal exploiter was simply replaced by the capitalist exploiter"[33] during the rise of capitalism was profoundly wrong—wrong in seeing a mere replacement. What really happened was the emergence of a new class of people with economic clout and political voice who countered the feudal lords, not to mention their new set of priorities and new ways of pursuing them. Over time, as profitability of enterprises attracted new entrepreneurs and additional technological innovations added to the number of entrepreneurs, power became less concentrated.

As noted, feudal lords—who possessed capital in the pre-capitalist era— rarely became industrialists themselves. There is evidence that some feudal lords became industrialists in Germany, a country that entered the industrial revolution later than, say, England, but elsewhere there is no significant evidence of feudal lords turning into industrialists.[34] Perhaps only after the industrialist approach proved to be rewarding in England did the feudal lords adjust their outlook in Germany. This is similar to the current experience, whereby successful companies are routinely unsuccessful in capitalizing on disruptive technologies that bring new value propositions to market.[35] This happens because their resources and outlook are geared towards a different set of priorities than the one required to nurture and exploit new technologies. In short, new ways of doing things mean new players, necessarily disrupting the old order and increasing, however small, in checks and balances. Checks and balances do increase because one influential person rarely replaces another; the society simply increases the number of influential people. Even when a new technology allows a new business to completely replace an old one, it is only in rare cases that the owner of the old business vanishes from the circle of influence.

The emergence of Internet Service Providers (ISPs) is a recent example of how technological innovations shift power. In this case, it is a shift from government-owned telecom monopolies to private entrepreneurs. This is particularly interesting because governments in poor countries rarely give away their turf if at all. ISPs appeared throughout developing countries relatively rapidly (relative to the time it had taken for the same number of telephones to appear) due to low cost of equipment and the existing populations of cheap and useful personal computers. The advent of ISPs has been so rapid that governments in developing countries were caught by surprise and, thus, had no laws in place to stop private initiatives. While the ISPs may now be subject to some rules and regulations, in most countries, they found initial footholds due to unprepared regulatory environments. In addition, government organizations lacked the capacity to handle new technologies on their own anyway. Ignorance also led government organizations to underestimate their potential impact at least in the early stages and let these technologies slip out of their hands. To see how vested interests can shift and move mountains, one can note the "bold deregulation of the telecom industry" in India in August 2000.[36] In India, where the state machinery has proved itself very reluctant to privatize state owned enterprises, the change did not occur until enough people, some powerful, joined the digital revolution.

One could argue that the rich and powerful tend to acquire new technologies and become even more rich and powerful. While this may have some truth in general, the impact of the digital revolution could be quite different because of the new possibilities of access and vigilance. Digital technologies are rather unusual due to their relentless price decline accompanied with an equally relentless increase in computing power, an effect described by Moore's law.[37] This increase in power also means a substantial future increase in the ease of using digital tools and a reduction in the skills needed to use them. The second factor that makes them unusual is that they have genuine global reach through the World Wide Web. That is, intellectual products can be shipped over great distances with virtually no physical constraints. These factors together mean that the technology, by its very nature, is becoming more accessible to the poor in terms of affordability, proximity and necessary skills.

And access leads to empowerment. Due to lower prices of computing equipment and the low cost of connectivity, small companies in poor countries are capable of delivering programming services to companies in richer countries. This is already giving rise to a new class of entrepreneurs—a class that would only increase in size over time—who may alter the structure of vested interests in poor countries. A young college graduate in a poor country could start a programming business with relatively little capital as a "virtual immigrant" by sending his products to companies in rich countries. Since productions in electronic form can be "shipped" instantly, little intervention, if any, would be possible between the producer and the buyer. In effect, these young entrepreneurs are already bypassing the old vested interests and would challenge such interests in tomorrow's politics.

For people in non-digital businesses, connecting with their customers and suppliers (domestic or international) through the inexpensive Internet enhances their capabilities considerably. Even at the lowest level, the spread of simple technologies like cellular telephones—in places where no phone lines have ever been laid—is making people more productive and empowered. If poverty have made them silent, such empowerment may give them a voice.

Access by a large number of people and negligible costs of connecting create new possibilities of self-organizing and vigilance by people.

According to Bill Gates, the founder of Microsoft, the single most important event in the digital revolution was the creation of personal computers that unleashed creativity and connectivity among millions of people.[38] Prior to this, computing power was confined to the hands of powerful organizations that could afford mainframe computers. This event alone shifted the relative power balance between individuals and large organizations, including governments, in favor of people. Although, at this point, the percentage of people having access to computing in poor countries is small, the number is increasing rapidly thanks to the continued decline in prices. Consequently, vast possibilities of connectivity have emerged throughout the world. The people-to-people connections—combined with a significant increase in trans-national non-governmental organizations, increased clout of financial markets, and increased capability of media have created a general devolution of authority of governments, bringing them nearer to peoples. The reason authorities would be nearer to peoples is the increased possibilities of vigilance by people directly on governments, businesses, and other organizations.

Technologies that have historically empowered ordinary citizens to be more productive have enhanced governance in the past. Simple innovations such as water mills, eyeglasses and mechanical clocks have empowered many relatively ordinary citizens in Europe since the Middle Ages.[39] This enabled many entrepreneurs to emerge from the bottom, which in turn gave birth to even more innovations. These entrepreneurs with sufficient economic and political voice pressed for and obtained property rights and rule of law from the political authorities. The political authorities in Europe, on the other hand, since the fall of Rome, happened to have been fragmented and small, and had to compromise with these entrepreneurs for them to survive. "Despotism abounded in Europe, too, but …[it was] mitigated by law, by territorial partition, and within states by division of power between the center (the crown) and local seignorial authority. Fragmentation gave rise to competition, and competition favored good care of good subjects. Treat them badly and they might go elsewhere."[40] While information technologies may not be fragmenting countries, the effective reduction of distance between authority and people could nonetheless be comparable. By extending peoples' reach into organizations (be they governmental or non-governmental), databases, media, and other human beings, people are getting closer to authorities.

While in Europe authority devolved for political reasons when separately technologies empowered people, the digital technologies now due to their very nature are initiating both a global devolution of authority and a global evolution of empowerment.

ACCESS LEADS TO EMPOWERMENT AND HIGHER DECIBELS.

As noted earlier, simple innovations, such as water mills, eyeglasses, and mechanical clocks, empowered many relatively ordinary citizens to form an entrepreneurial class in Europe since the Middle Ages. This new class—distinct from the nobility and larger in number—created a counter balance against the feudal lords. The key, however, was relatively manageable costs of these technologies and their ability to increase productivity. Digital technologies of today have similar characteristics—not only do prices continue to decline and the machines become easier to use, new forms of connectivity create new possibilities of combining skills and resources.

Digital tools and new business models allow ordinary citizens to be more productive, more informed, and bypass restrictive regimes. In other words, the digital revolution is giving birth to new "water mills," "eyeglasses", and "mechanical clocks" that allow the relatively poor to gain certain economic advantages.

In addition to price declines and other reasons making these tools potentially accessible to a large number of people, there are at least three reasons why digital technologies can help ordinary people in poor countries. First, they are producer tools, not consumer goods. Their very nature helps people be more productive, coordinate their activities, and analyze and monitor problems more thoroughly. Second, they are bypassing tools. They can allow direct access to information, cutting layers of bureaucracies—the layers that have been obstructing people. Low-cost Internet connections bypass high-priced telephone calls. Sending a production over the wire bypasses the harassment of corrupt customs officials. Third, digital technologies are able to compensate for the weaknesses in poor countries. A cell phone can overcome at least some of the problems of a bad road. Voice recognition can at least partially overcome problems of illiteracy. Email and the web are overcoming an array of things, including the high cost of telephones. Absence of libraries or research centers is compensated for by easily accessible information through the web. Consider

> ...the possible use of the Internet to change the lives of hundreds of millions of villagers. In the past, many would sell their produce to traders at whatever price was offered. Now the telephone and the Internet give them instant information on relative prices in different market towns, greatly improving their bargaining power...Villagers also pay hefty bribes to officials to see land records. But the Internet should allow them to download such information instantly and discover when the records have been tampered with. Villagers seeking work abroad sometimes have to pay touts and labor contractors large sums to get a passport. With access to an Internet link they may be able to download a passport application form and submit it by post... Unsurprisingly, the state bureaucracies oppose the computerization of government records because they stand to lose from such openness. Yet the process may now be unstoppable. In some villages, rural-Indian versions of Internet cafes are already springing up.[41]

In Bangladesh, GrameenPhone, working in collaboration with Grameen Bank, has brought cellular telephony already to 3,000 villages that did not have telephones before. The program is expanding, adding 100-200 new villages every month. In each of these villages, a poor person obtains a micro-loan from Grameen Bank, purchases a handset, and starts retailing telephone services in his/her village. This creates a small business for a poor person and provides connectivity to a whole village, an average of 2,000 people. While on average about 70 people become regular customers of each village phone, the whole village becomes connected to the outside world, receiving information on market prices, doctors, job opportunities, wellbeing of relatives, etc. In addition to being economically empowered due to the availability of such valuable information, people feel socially empowered as well. A crime can be quickly reported to the police or newspapers. Without the digital revolution, a commercial enterprise like GrameenPhone would not have been possible.

AUTHORITY COMES NEARER THROUGH INCREASED VIGILANCE.

If the state has enjoyed too much power relative to the people and other organizations and contributed to poor governance, technology may have arrived as the white knight to challenge the state by empowering the media, non-governmental organizations, financial markets, multinational companies, and individuals. For instance, during the Gulf War in 1991, the US government—the most powerful one in the world—acknowledged that sometime it got battlefield information from the private television channel CNN, powered by satellite communication.

It has been widely noted that, "Nongovernmental organizations (NGOs) are invading areas that used to be reserved for national politicians. Some NGOs, such as the Soros Foundation, Amnesty International, Doctors without Borders, and Alert International, already command resources that dwarf those available to the states in which they operate; and the imbalance is likely to get bigger still, particularly given the fact that first-world activists are rather more technologically savvy than third-world bureaucrats."[42] Technology is also "shifting financial clout from states to the market with its offer of unprecedented speed in transactions—states cannot match market reaction times measured in seconds—and its dissemination of financial information to a broad range of players."[43]

Large multinational companies, also empowered by technology, are taking power away from nation states.[44] Countries often compete and, consequently, change policies—to attract investments from large companies. Moreover, "Global markets in finance and advanced services partly operate through a 'regulatory' umbrella that is not state centered but market centered."[45] However, because of the increased ability of the public—again due to technology—to be vigilant about corporate behavior, corporations increasingly self-regulate, which has the added benefit of avoiding cumbersome involvement with government bureaucracies. Brand name and corporate image are important corporate assets, and large companies, by definition, have big reputations to protect. Increased global connectivity makes companies suffer throughout the world for misdeeds carried out in a single region, no matter how remote. As a result, corporations are not necessarily escaping regulation, but rather the regulatory power is shifting somewhat from the hands of the state to the hands of media, non-governmental organizations and people.

Increased connectivity empowers the peoples vis-à-vis their governments in at least five ways.[46] First, connected people can more easily and efficiently organize themselves. Second, multiple sources of information reduce the chances of people being deceived. Third, as private companies increasingly adopt digital technologies and provide efficient services, archaic government processes appear increasingly incompetent thereby creating pressure for change. Fourth, seeing how people in other countries live makes people demand fairer and better treatment at home. Fifth, people connected across borders make it difficult for regimes to demonize foreign peoples. Demonizing human beings in other countries and creating a perceived threat from outside are old-fashioned techniques for regimes to distract people from domestic problems that vested interests prevent them from solving.

To see how increased connectivity enhances peoples' fundamental ability to self-organize, consider Iran and China. "In Iran, where service has more than doubled since 1990, the telephone was pivotal in the stunning upset victory in May [1997] of moderate president Mohammed Khatami. ...word of mouth...campaign brought millions of Iranians to the polls who had never voted before—particularly women and young people who rely heavily on telephones because of limited public forums for communications."[47] In China, the "state constraints are powerful, but not comprehensive. The government felt angry and foolish when...10,000 or more followers of the Falun Gong suddenly surrounded the compound in Beijing where the top leaders live. ...organized in large part by e-mail that the government could not detect."[48]

This is why dictators typically keep telephone networks or other methods of connectivity to a minimum. Due to satellite television and the spread of the Internet, for instance, most developing countries now have access to information about and from the outside world. With various degrees of limitations, in aggregate there has been a vast increase in telecommunication facilities in the developing world just over the last decade because the digital revolution is constantly opening up new and less expensive possibilities of connecting. Once various forms of connectivity are unleashed, they feed on themselves. People understand how their lives improve and demand more. The genie keeps growing.

Changing Global Vested Interests Eases Access and Vigilance.

Vested interests rule. But as history shows, they are not necessarily bad. Just as the vested interests of merchants in England, and, later, business interests in East Asia set off a virtuous cycle of prosperity and better governance, powerful global economic interests exist today to repeat such virtuous cycles. Long-term investors and global business leaders know that their prosperity is tied to the prosperity of their customers and employees, increasingly worldwide. Globalization is shifting power from states to companies, non-governmental organizations and peoples; but more importantly, the fates of all entities are increasingly being tied together, and all entities are subject to increased vigilance by people, directly or indirectly. Business communities are also beginning to see poor countries not as targets for aid and charity or as origins of natural resources, but as areas with potential for commercial give-and-take, not much different from rich communities. According to Carly Fiorina, Chairman and Chief Executive Officer of Hewlett-Packard:

> ...the potential for economic growth in emerging market economies has never been greater. OECD statistics show that spending on information technologies in these economies is growing at a rate twice as fast as in the industrialized world...although it started from a lower base...Through such investments, the world's poorest countries can skip directly to the digital world. And in this wired world, they can reach beyond present boundaries...to learn new agricultural techniques...to find best medical practices...to buy and sell their commodities, goods and services.[49]

One clear economic reason is Moore's Law. If computing power is doubling every 18 months, computing power 100 times greater will be available at today's costs 10 years from now. If that makes today's personal computers available at one-third or one-fourth today's price, vast markets would open up in the poor countries.

Somewhat related to this price phenomenon are the specific economics of digital hardware and software that make the interdependence between the rich and poor countries fundamentally different from that in the past. Microsoft and Mercedes have completely different cost structures to sell their respective wares in Myanmar (Burma). Digital tools require a massive amount of investment to develop but very little costs to reproduce. Higher volume sales have negligible additional manufacturing costs, increasing margins to Microsoft. This economics is also true, only to a slightly lesser extent, for digital hardware manufacturers. It is partially true, and increasingly truer, for traditional manufactured products, such as the Mercedes cars where microchips are increasingly employed. As a result, digital industries, the more powerful parts of advanced economies of today (considering, the market capitalization of Microsoft relative to Daimler-Chrysler, the owner of Mercedes), should be pushing to penetrate markets in poor countries more than traditional manufacturers have done in the past. The powerful, high-tech companies are feeling the poverty, illiteracy, and lack of infrastructure of poor countries far more acutely than the traditional manufacturers of rich countries do. If these problems did not exist, there would be hundreds of millions more profit-producing customers for high-tech companies at little cost, i.e. marketing but not manufacturing cost.

The other side of high development costs of digital technologies is also interesting. The high development costs are pushing companies in rich countries to subcontract part of development to companies in poor countries, increasing the possibilities of effective technology transfer, i.e., through a genuinely participatory process. This too was not as true in traditional manufacturing, because co-production and co-design are now fundamentally easier with instant and comprehensive communication and the instantaneous transport of products. In addition to economic incentives, there could be increased political pressure for work done by "virtual immigrants" due to rapidly changing demographics in developed countries. "Just thirty years from now, one in four people in the developed world will be ages 65 or older, up from one in seven today,"[46] putting a huge strain on any social security system that attempts to financially support the retired population from the incomes of the working population. Possible taxes on the incomes of "virtual immigrants" may turn out to be an attractive source of revenues for rich governments.

An important aspect of digital tools is their utility to human minds and brains. The more these tools are sold, the more minds are connected and the more brains are activated, with automatic implication of empowered and organized citizenry. As powerful vested interests attempt to sell these technologies to wider and wider circles, education in poor countries will be part of the vested interests, despite the fact that some of these technologies could actually be used by people who are not even literate. The sale of products to the individual level is also to be contrasted with large development projects of the last 50 years (e.g. dams, power plants, and airports), where the buyers were usually governments with associated room for politics and corrupt practices. While developing countries need large infrastructure projects, the big incentives they create motivate powerful entities to pursue projects irrespective of their actual utility on the ground. Because of these reasons, a shift of exports (from rich to poor countries) towards more digital tools would bring about positive changes as people's consumption power (education, skills, etc.) and purchasing power become relevant to exporters.

Furthermore, powerful companies and investment communities in rich countries are also realizing that poor governance has not only limited their market potential and production possibilities, it also has limited the scope of investments. As savings pile up in rich countries because capital avoids inhospitable investment climates where investment is ironically most desperately needed, it is the inferior governance in poor countries that is significantly eating into the potential return for investors in rich countries. This irony has been in existence for a long time, but the digital and communication revolutions make it more visible, more acutely felt, and solvable.

With these new economic forces, powerful companies in rich countries increasingly ask their governments to help them open markets and improve governance worldwide. These powerful companies and their home governments have considerable leverage with governments in poor countries. If this leverage—whose ineffective use in the past has contributed to worsening governance— is used wisely, it could contribute to improving governance. If the governments in rich and poor countries focus on serving their peoples—and collaborate in doing just that—they will add tailwinds to the economic and social progress already being unleashed by the digital revolution. If the governments in rich and poor countries instead focus on their narrow short-term interests, they will only add headwinds that slow the process. But, either way, the process is unstoppable. The process will transform governments towards serving peoples.

ENDNOTES

1.   There are exceptions, whereby rulers—autocratic or otherwise—voluntarily solve people's problems (e.g. Emperor Ashoka in India of third century BC, Emperor Meiji in late nineteenth century Japan, and Lee Kuan Yew in recent Singapore) without having to meet demands from below. These unexpected aberrations do not necessarily illuminate the natural processes that produce accountable governments.

2.   Barbara Crossette, "Making Room for the Poor In a Global Economy," *The New York Times*, April 16, 2000, Section 4, page 1.

3.   *Ibid.*

4.   Jessica T. Mathew, "Power Shift," *Foreign Affairs*, January/February 1997, p. 51.

5.   Hernando de Soto finds that "being free from the costs and nuisance of the extralegal sector generally compensates for paying taxes." Hernando de Soto, *The Mystery of Capital* (New York: Basic Books, 2000) p. 155.

6.   Nayan Chanda, "Gates and Gandhi," *Far Eastern Economic Review*, August 24, 2000, p. 60.

7.   Minxin Pei, "Will China Become Another Indonesia?" *Foreign Policy*, Fall 1999, p. 94.

8.   James D. Wolfensohn, "Forward," *The World Development Report 1997* (The World Bank: Washington DC, 1997).

9.   Fredrich A. Hayek, *The Fatal Conceit* (Chicago: The University of Chicago Press, 1988) p. 45, refers to Jean Baechler, *The Origin of Capitalism* (Oxford: Blackwells, 1975) p.77.

10. *The Economist*, "Survey on The New Economy," September 23-29, 2000, p. 39.

11. Daniel R. Fuslid, *The Age of the Economist* (Reading, MA: Addison-Wesley, 1999) p. 61.

12. For example, Amartya Sen [*Development As Freedom* (New York: Alfred A. Knopf, 1999)], the winner of the 1998 Nobel Prize in economics, elaborates extensively and eloquently on the importance of freedom in people's lives, and by increasing freedom—which is inextricably linked to good governance—a country can make progress. Thomas Friedman [*The Lexus and the Olive Tree* (New York: Anchor Books, 2000)] explains that if governments adopted right policies, their countries could capitalize on the forces of globalization and enjoy economic growth. Economic growth, according to the World Bank, leads to reduction in poverty.

13. See, for example, Mason et al., *The Economic and Social Modernization of the Republic of Korea* (Cambridge: Harvard University Press, 1980); Tom Gold, *State and Society in the Taiwan Miracle* (New York: M. E. Sharpe, 1986); Chalmers Johnson, *MITI and the Japanese Miracle: The Growth of Industrial Policy, 1925-1975* (Stanford, Calif.:Stanford University Press, 1982).

14. Daniel Fuslid, p. 14.

15. Thomas Homer-Dixon, *The Ingenuity Gap* (New York: Alfred K. Knopf, 2000) p. 370.

16. Niccolo Machiavelli, *The Prince* (New York: Bantam Books, 1966) p. 111.

17. Brink Lindsey, "Big Mistake," *Reason*, February 1996, quoted in Thomas Petzinger, Jr., *The New Pioneers* (New York: Simon and Schuster, 1999) p.7.

18. Robert Conquest finds that the Soviet form of communism was pursued and implemented by people of high social and academic standing, who were not the "proletariat" themselves. Also, many who were expressly dedicated in the West to studying the Soviet phenomenon failed to understand the extent of the problem there despite the availability of numerous indications and information. See Robert Conquest, *Reflections on a Ravaged Century* (New York: W. W. Norton & Company, 2000).

19. David S. Landes, *The Wealth and Poverty of Nations* (New York: W. W. Norton & Company, 1998) p. 44.

20. Jeffrey Sachs, "International Economics: Unlocking the Mysteries of Globalization," *Foreign Policy*, Spring 1998, p. 99.

21. The World Bank, *The World Development Report 2000/2001: Attacking Poverty* (Oxford: Oxford University Press, 2000) p. 51.

22. David Bornstein, *The Price of a Dream* (New York: Simon & Schuster, 1996) p. 44.

23. John Seely Brown and Paul Duguid, *The Social Life of Information* (Boston, MA: Harvard Business School Press, 2000) p. 5.

24. Antonio Damasio, *The Feeling of What Happens* (San Diego: Harcourt, 1999). Also see Antonio Damasio, *Descartes's Error* (New York: Avon Books, Inc, 1994).

25. An apparent conclusion made in a gathering of scholars in Washington, DC in 1997. See Jerome Glenn and Theodore Gordon, eds., *State of the Future: Implication for Action Today* (Washington DC: American Council for the United Nations University, 1997) p. 29, Quoted from Homer-Dixon, p. 28.

26. Adam Smith, *An Inquiry Into the Nature and Causes of the Wealth of Nations* (Chicago: William Benton, 1952) p. 7.

27. The damages that can be caused by an increase in state power were understood by the founders of the United States of America who devised specific means, including the Constitution, to keep state power in check.

28   Thomas Petzinger, Jr., *The New Pioneers* (New York: Simon & Schuster, 1999) p. 20.

29. Mick Moore, "Toward a Useful Consensus?" *IDS Bulletin*, 29(2), 1998, p.47.

30. According to David Dollar (Research Manager, Development Research Group at the World Bank), "Much assistance is allocated to donors' strategic allies, who are often middle income countries, not the truly poor." Nancy Bearg Dyke, ed., *The International Poverty Gap: Investing in People and Technology to Build Sustainable Pathways Out* (Washington, DC: The

Aspen Institute, 2000) p. 104. See also p. 102 where Dollar writes that "allocation of aid is very political."

31. In 1956, Robert Solow and T. W. Swan developed a simple model of economic growth as a function of capital and labor, implying that an increase in capital leads to higher growth. In the last ten years, economists have challenged this simple model and brought other factors, such as technological innovations, into account.

32. David Dollar, "How Policy Reform and Effective Aid Can Reduce Global Poverty," in Nancy Bearg Dyke, ed., *The International Poverty Gap: Investing in People and Technology to Build Sustainable Pathways Out* (Washington, DC: The Aspen Institute, 2000).

33. Joseph A. Schumpeter, *Capitalism, Socialism and Democracy* (New York: Harpar & Brothers, 1942) p. 17.

34. *Ibid.*

35. Clayton Christiansen, *The Innovator's Dilemma: When New Technologies Cause Great Firms to Fail* (New York: HarperBusiness, 2000).

36. *Ibid.*

37. Gordon Moore, the founder of Intel Corporation, argued that computing power doubles every 18 months at constant cost. This implies computing power increasing by a factor of four in three years, or a factor of 64 in nine years, or nearly a factor of 100 in ten years.

38. Bill Gates said this during the question and answer period after his speech on October 18, 2000, in the conference titled Creating Digital Dividends in Seattle, Washington.

39. Landes. pp. 45-59.

40. Landes, p. 36.

41. *The Economist,* "When India Wires Up," July 22, 2000, p. 40.

42. John Mickelethwait and Adrian Wooldridge, *A Future Perfect* (New York: Crown Business, 2000) p. 155.

43. Mathews, p. 57.

44. Saskia Sassen, *Losing Control: Sovereignty in an Age of Globalization* (New York: Columbia University Press, 1996).

45. Saskia Sassen, *Globalization and Its Discontents* (New York: The New Press, 1998) p. XXVII.

46. For a similar discussion, see Frances Cairncross, *The Death of Distance* (Boston: Harvard Business School Press, 1997) p.257-279.

47. Robin Wright, "Cellular Phones Answers Rural Areas Needs" *Los Angeles Times,* November 10, 1997.

48. *The Economist,* "The Flies Swarm In," July 22, 2000, p. 28.

49. Carly Fiorina, Chairman and CEO of Hewlett Packard, "The Digital Ecosystem," a speech delivered at a conference titled "Creating Digital Dividends," Seattle, WA, October 16, 2000.

50. Peter G. Peterson, *Gray Dawn* (New York: Times Books, 1999) p.13.

Empowering the Poor: The Role of Technology*

By Edith Ssempala**
August 19, 2000

Editor's note: We asked Ambassador Ssempala to outline in remarks for the conference her views on the role of technology—especially what works—in poverty alleviation, as seen from a developing country perspective. Her key points are presented here.

Technology has a critical role in fighting poverty and in empowering the poor to uplift their standard of living.

There are two kinds of technology:

1. Appropriate Technology

This is a technology that can be operated and maintained by people who are not educated and may have basic or no skills. There are success stories in Uganda where appropriate technology has empowered poor people, especially women. For example, in Eastern Uganda a low-cost building project using appropriate technology has given poor women an opportunity to make building materials, use some of the materials to build better houses for their families, sell the surplus, and generate some income. These women, who had at one time been forced into prostitution by poverty, are now respected and productive members of their community, and they are no longer prostitutes.

2. High-Tech

High-tech holds a lot of promise for the poor. However, for the time being most of the technology is not accessible because of lack of infrastructure, especially electricity. E-mail, the Internet, telemedicine, and similar technologies would be very useful in empowering the poor if these technologies were accessible and affordable. Since

---

* Remarks presented at the Aspen Institute International Peace, Security & Prosperity conference "Alleviating Global Poverty: Technology for Economic and Social Uplift," August 18-20, 2000.

** Edith Ssempala is the Ambassador of Uganda to the United States.

investments in infrastructure are costly and therefore rural electrification in developing countries will take time, wireless communication is the answer. In Uganda, cellular telephones have created an enormous opportunity for the poor by enabling them to communicate and run their small businesses more efficiently.

Entrepreneurship

Another factor, which is not technology related, and yet is really the source of empowerment, is what I call mental empowerment. Poor people can do a lot to help themselves if they believe they can. Even with little skills and no capital, it is possible to improve one's condition. I know people in Uganda who started by selling matchboxes and are now industrialists. The power behind their success is not high education, not financial capital; it is their mental capital, "entrepreneurship."

I believe that a combination of entrepreneurship, appropriate technology, and high-tech would go a long way in empowering the poor people to uplift themselves from poverty.

Scaling up Microfinance and Poverty Reduction*

By Jacques Attali**
August 19, 2000

Many of the questions that have been raised thus far in this conference on the role of technology in reducing global poverty have been about scalability and local experience in general. Can we help people to use their own initiative to fight against poverty? Can we use new technology to create jobs? Creating jobs is certainly important at a moment when democracy is generating enormous new demand for jobs now and in future decades. Is there an association between creation of jobs and the fight against poverty?

I believe that microfinance is the key element in answering these questions. My experience over the last 2½ years tells me that microfinance and the Internet are similar to two separate chemical products which are less powerful when separate, but when mixed together form a chemical bond and result in an entirely new compound with distinct properties and increased potential. Similarly, when mixed together, microfinance and the Internet create a new supertool that is a powerhouse of job creation and poverty alleviation. Microfinance is a process through which people create their own jobs using very small loans provided by banks. The Internet is the ingredient—the technology—that can scale up microfinance so that it reaches a broader consumer base, empowering millions more individuals and decreasing poverty.

In explaining the impressive potential of microfinance and the Internet, I will concentrate on my experience acquired at PlaNet Finance, an organization created after the first Aspen Institute global poverty conference 3½ years ago in England. PlaNet Finance is an international non-profit institution aimed at reducing poverty by supporting financial organizations that support the poor. It does so by providing resources over the Internet.

* Remarks presented at The Aspen Institute International Peace, Security & Prosperity Program conference, "Alleviating Poverty: Technology for Economic and Social Uplift," August 18-20, 2000.

** Jacques Attali is President of PlaNet Finance, President of Attali & Associés, and former President of the European Bank for Reconstruction and Development.

I would just like to digress a moment to remind all of you what microfinance is about. Microfinance is a process through which people create their own jobs using very small loans provided by banks. The banks or microfinance institutions (MFIs) loan the money to individuals without a guarantee or collateral. With such a loan, a person can start an enterprise that will earn money and perhaps grow and create additional jobs. People use their own initiative to raise their quality of life and fight their poverty. For instance, a woman who buys one sewing machine with her microloan can earn enough money to send her children to school and also spawn a microenterprise employing several village women.

Today, around the world there exist 7,000 MFIs or microfinance banks. These 7,000 microfinance banks have 5 million clients. All in all, the MFIs are very efficient. The rate of loan repayment, 97%, is better than with commercial banks. The efficiency in the rate of return is excellent, too. The capacity of these institutions to help people get out of poverty is amazing; according to our statistics, people are escaping poverty through these programs. For example, Mohammad Yunus, the inventor of microcredit, created in Bangladesh the first bank for the poor in 1983. As a result, 30% of the 2.5 million people who have received loans have managed to escape from poverty.

The number of potential microfinance clients worldwide is estimated at 500 million.[1] The question is how to go from the current 15 million to 500 million. The answer, in my view, is the Internet. The Internet is the leverage to bring microfinance to scale, not by providing Internet to each client, but, by giving the microfinance institutions two things: first, access to the Internet in order to allow them to be professionalized and available to the markets; and second, access to resources.

That is exactly what we are trying to do with PlaNet Finance, the institution that I created in 1998 and which is now working in Paris. Today, we have 100 people and offices in 10 countries worldwide. It is financed by private sponsors, some of them around this table; by international institutions, some also represented around this table; and by a number of computer companies. PlaNet Finance is non-profit, and it is my goal that it be self-sustaining within the next two years. We try to provide full services through the Internet to help microfinance institutions as they work with more than 15 million clients, with a goal of 100 million in the next seven years, a common target accepted by the international community.[2] The longer-term goal is 500 million clients. The avenue to meeting these goals is channeling commercial bank funds to microfinance. If for seven years US$20 million a year of commercial money could be channeled to microfinance, the number of microfinance clients could jump from 15 million to 100 million. That means 85 million additional micro-entrepreneurs working their way out of poverty.

PlaNet Finance provides a comprehensive set of services through the Internet to develop microfinance. The first service is exchange of information between institutions. We are the largest Internet bank network. When someone in Brazil wants to know the best experience in terms of microfinancing in a rural area, he can find out through our website.[3] Donors, as well as anyone else, can learn about existing institutions. We also advise financial institutions and private banks in order to create new microfinance institutions. We are discussing with the European Investment Bank creating microfinance subsidiaries; and we have been asked by governments in the Middle East and by the Chinese government to help create the beginnings of institutional infrastructure for microfinance entities.

The second service we provide is training for people in the microfinance institutions. We have a university where we provide off-line and online training in two dimensions: one is new technology and the second is banking competence specific to microfinance. The PlaNet University can provide training on new technologies as well as specific accounting techniques on the Internet to professionalize institutions.

The third dimension is to provide these institutions with more computers and then additional websites to plug them into the market.

Another essential dimension is to give the market confidence about these institutions—to have these institutions be known by the market through rating. But, the traditional rating agencies are not rating the microfinance institutions. We have created a specific rating instrument for this, and we are one of two or three organizations around the world rating these institutions. The purpose is to provide them advice and a professional rating that will lead to access to the global funding that can be available once they are known to be professionally rated and profitable. The PlaNet Finance rating system is working extremely well, and now we have a tremendous number of institutions asking to be rated. They have to have faith in our system in order to make that request. For example, in Benin, Association pour la Promotion et l'Appui au Développement des Micro Entreprises (PADME) was evaluated by PlaNet Finance and received a favorable grade. Based on this analysis, the Financial Bank, Benin granted PADME a cash credit amounting to US$1 million. This new resource made it possible for PADME to provide loans to 2,000 new clients, with an average loan amount of US$500.

PlaNet Finance also has its own funding system; we fund microfinance institutions through the Internet. We can donate to them, as we have over US$10 million available for this program. We also have a development department.

Finally, we have Ethic Village, which sells, without fee, products created by the clients of microfinance institutions. Ethic Village's purpose is to be able to guarantee a fair, lasting, direct, transparent, and quality trade. We do so by:

- defining with the producer a price that guarantees him a fair income;
- committing ourselves to establishing a long-term trade relationship taking into account his social, environmental and economic situation requirements
- establishing a one-to-one relationship between producer and consumer in order to promote exchanges and mutual respect;
- providing complete information concerning the products, their ori-gin, and their life story;
- selecting quality products and offering the best service possible to the consumer.

In summary, it is amazing to see how well it all works, but we at PlaNet Finance are limited by the amount of resources in place, as is microfinance everywhere. I would say that the PlaNet Finance rating instrument, the fund, and the university will be self-sustaining in the next few years. Then the larger challenge is to ensure that these and other activities will assist microfinance institutions so they can attract substantially more commercial funding to scale up job creation among the world's poor through microfinance.

ENDNOTES

1. "Meeting the Challenge of Reaching the Poorest." 1999 Microcredit Summit Campaign Report, available: <http://www.microcreditsummit.org/campaigns/report99.htm>.
2. Ibid.
3. See http://www.planetfinance.org

Poverty Alleviation and Renewable Energy in a Sustainable Context*

By Helena Chum and Ralph Overend**

Poverty has been described as "the greatest threat to political stability, social cohesion and environmental health on the planet." As we move into the 21st century, approximately 4.4 billion people (of a total world population of 6 billion) live in developing countries and one-third of the world's population live on less than a dollar a day. Often-quoted figures are that 2 billion persons are without electricity, 1 billion lack access to clean drinking water, 2.5 billion do not have adequate sanitation, and 800 million are without sufficient food. Despite much effort, the number of disadvantaged people is growing each year. It is time to think about new models of poverty alleviation to address the problems that affect the lives of almost half the world's population. Science and technology, especially in renewable energy and systems, can help alleviate poverty by creating conditions for sustainable and environmentally conscious economic growth. This paper describes proven methods and initiatives that can be replicated throughout the developing world.

Meeting Basic Needs

The estimated typical daily needs of humans to satisfy minimum standards of opportunity are:
- Nutrition: 2,500 kcal and 80 to 100 grams of protein per person per day
- Shelter: approximately 7 square meters per person
- Clean drinking water: 50 liters/day/person
- Access to safe sanitation
- Access to health care
- Access to education and training with a goal of 12 years of basic education for each student

* Paper prepared for the Aspen Institute International Peace, Security & Prosperity Program conference, "Alleviating Global Poverty: Technology for Economic and Social Uplift," August 18-20, 2000.

** Helena Chum is the Director of the Bioenergy Systems Center, National Renewable Energy Laboratory (USA). Ralph Overend is a Research Fellow at the National Renewable Energy Laboratory (USA).

- Reliable, adequate energy services for daily living and productive use
- Access to information. This category grows in importance but may be beyond minimum standards.

Only by providing all of these, can we hope to improve the quality of life, which is measured by such coarse indicators as: infant mortality, literacy, and life expectancy. All too often the solution to meeting these needs consists of large projects focused on only one of the developmental needs in a given community or nation. As a result, the urban poor continue to live in favelas (slum conditions) without proper sanitation or even minimal services, such as public transportation for travel to work. In the countryside, where more than half the developing world lives, the situation is often much worse. This is especially true in plantation crop economies, where malnutrition and hunger are common.

Poverty alleviation and sustainable human development are closely linked. Sustainable human development is development that not only generates economic growth but distributes its benefits equitably, that regenerates the environment rather than destroying it, that empowers people rather than marginalizing them. It is development that gives the poor greater control, enlarging their choices and opportunities and providing for their participation in decisions that affect their lives. It is development that is pro-people, pro-nature and pro-women.[1]

The basic needs of the poor will be met in the long run by increasing their productive capacity. The degree to which technology is successfully utilized directly affects productivity.[2]

Science and technology, especially in the area of renewable energy, have played a role in many of the areas key to poverty alleviation, such as:

- Basic social services (education and primary health care). Renewable technologies have brought improvement for the poor in rural villages, for example, by enabling night school courses to be held using lamps. Primary health care has improved through powering refrigeration units for vaccines and other medical supplies.
- Agricultural reform. Biomass technologies have been enabling the production of food and feed in conjunction with productive use of residues for energy and products. Much more can and should be done in this area, which is a basic subject of this paper.
- Credit to open markets. Renewable energy has allowed many villages to take advantage of credit to develop productive activities. These loans are slowly improving the economic conditions of these villages. For example, providing electrification to poor villages through the first credit sales of photovoltaic (PV) systems allowed

Biomass: plants, crops, and trees converted into fuels and by-products

village saloons and other businesses to generate more revenue or step up production by remaining open later into the night.[3]

- Employment for sustainable livelihood. Between 1978 and 1995, integrated use of biomass in China created jobs and reduced the number of poor from 250 million to 80 million.[4] China may be able to use its rural resources (residues from agriculture, people in the rural areas, food/feed and, energy) to continue along the path of rural development.

- Participation in economic development design. The more the poor participate in the development of programs designed to help them lift themselves out of poverty, the more successful they will be. For instance, what should be the priority order between making water available through pumping to a poor community or providing their homes with electricity? Without water, subsistence farming and additional development through agriculture is not possible. So, water pumping and water purification should be first. Then, electrifying those rural homes will help stem the flow of the rural poor to over-burdened urban areas.

By making these and other contributions of renewable energy to basic needs, one expects that:

- Basic quality of life will be improved for those excluded by the market, which then will advance their efforts to join the market economy at some point.
- Productivity and economic growth of the poor will increase.
- Environmental sustainability, as measured by reduced pressure on the eco-system, will be achieved.

Village Power

While there are sustainable city initiatives[5] that are improving the lot of the urban poor, there are fewer equivalent programs for the rural poor.[6] Some effective village-based development programs are ongoing, but much more remains to be done.[7] The particular anecdotal observations provided so far come from more than 10 years of village power experience of staff at NREL. Many initiatives around the world are continuing. If, as needed, the number of such initiatives is multipled, it could decrease rural poverty and at the same time increase economic opportunities for the rural poor.

Mindful of our agency's mission to lead the way toward a sustainable energy future, we at NREL started with energy—one basis for improving the quality of life. We examined its use in:

- Daily living – cooking, water heating, lighting, and space heating
- Commercial and industrial use of lighting, heating/cooling, refrigeration, and in manufacturing process heat

- Transportation and communications

NREL's village power focus has led to recognition of the applications of renewable energy in generating electricity, pumping water, and improving cooking fuel utilization efficiencies.[8] Applications of PV, wind power, small hydro, and biomass all play a role. Energy per se is of little use. Energy has to be associated with a productive use for the community to grow.

Renewable Energy Options

Global problems of energy supply are solved at the local level with renewables that draw their energy from the environment. Without irrigation, arid areas cannot sustain small hydroelectric and biomass options. Wind is not distributed uniformly, though new mapping and exploration techniques developed by NREL have revealed far greater potentials than previously thought. Fortunately, solar energy is available in most tropical locations. Even relatively cloudy locations can gather significant energy to power the photosynthesis of trees and grasses.

Delivery of energy to individual villages and their citizens is not easy because grid extension is often prohibitively expensive; and households may be widely scattered. NREL has developed the Hybrid Optimization Model for Electric Renewables for the cost assessment of PV, wind, small hydro, and hybrid fossil systems. NREL also offers tools, such as the Village Power Optimization Model for Renewables, that will optimize the distribution of power from a central source and account for houses that are too far from the mini-grid using solar home systems.

Estimates of energy needs vary, but one estimate places the need at approximately 0.5 kW/person for minimal development. This figure is based on representative populations and income indices.

One concept being developed for the Food and Agriculture Organization (FAO) by Nasir El Bassam is the Integrated Renewable Energy Farm (IREF)[9]. Designed for a village complex of about 3,000 persons, this energy form would include an energy plantation of 250 to 300 hectares producing food, fiber, and fuel. A combined heat and power unit and a bioethanol fuels plant are also included. Both wind and photovoltaic cells would augment the renewable energy supply. The multipurpose biomass crop proposed is sweet sorghum that will grow in both temperate and tropical zones in reasonably high yield with moderate inputs.

The delivery of electricity and energy services increasingly is moving to the private sector to energy service companies (ESCO) and their renewable and local variant, the renewable or rural energy service companies (RESCO). For this to work, the government (local, regional, or national) has to establish a franchise for the RESCO to service. The RESCO provides the capital, the installation, and the service including maintenance, and through its revenue collection will generate a return on the investment. This move to the private sector is part of a large-scale electricity industry reform that is changing the structure of national electricity services in both the industrial and developing worlds.

In the OECD the electricity restructuring changes have separated electricity generation, transmission, and distribution into separate companies and have given consumers choice over their electricity suppliers. Discerning consumers can now purchase green electricity from renewable sources. In developing countries the concern is that the disappearance of the national electricity company will delay the electrification of the regions currently not served. However, on a larger scale, biomass resources such as sugarcane bagasse, palm oil mills, wood processing, and pulp and paper production can now contribute to the electricity supply through the economical generation of both heat and power for their processes and export of renewable electricity to neighboring communities and the transmission grid. The opportunity for efficient use of fuels through combined heat and power or co-generation has been increased through the creation of competition at all levels of the electricity system.

Environmental Technologies

Environmental technologies are a developing area for biomass conversion and the production of useful energy. The largest existing systems are based on anaerobic digestion, either in specially designed processes for specific environmental problems or in landfills that are managed to capture the methane they naturally produce. Anaerobic digestion has been used for many years in the treatment of sewage and animal manure to mineralize the carbon and reduce the volume of waste sludge for disposal. In the mineralization process the carbon is converted into methane and carbon dioxide in about a 60:40 ratio by volume that depends on the material being digested. The processed bacteria and non-digested material remains as a sludge that can be returned to the soil if there are no heavy metals from the residue stream.

The biological processes of anaerobic digestion are mediated by the action of microorganisms that secrete enzymes utilized to break down biomass and produce a desired product. Since most biological processes are conducted in the liquid phase, they are ideally suited for water and wet solid residue treatments. A wide range of agricultural, industrial, and urban activities produce suitable streams for anaerobic treatment. Examples of residue streams with high organic loadings include intensive animal husbandry (excreta and bedding materials), food processing (sugar production, vegetable preparation), residue streams from breweries and distilleries, sludges from materials production such as from pulp and paper manufacture, pharmaceuticals manufacture, and sewage treatment. All of these processes have residue streams with high organic loadings. Without any treatment, these industries pollute watercourses and ground water with high loadings of biological and chemical oxygen demand and with large concentrations of nitrates, microbial contaminants, and pathogens.

Anaerobic digestion technology is able to convert a significant fraction of the organic loading in these residue streams into biogas, which has a heating value of about 50% of that of natural gas. The remaining solids (sludge) and liquor still have to be managed, sometimes by aerobic treatments to meet environmental requirements for release of water into the environment. The range of technologies to produce energy while treating these residues is almost as wide as the range of streams or substrates to be treated.

In the 1960's and 70's, the problem of water contamination was recognized. With the energy crisis of the early 1970's, increasing efforts have been put into anaerobic digestion technologies. However, it is only recently that the technologies have reached a stage of technological and economic viability that deployment has become feasible. Progress in these areas has increased the reliability or the effective time-on-stream of the applications. It has also improved the conversion efficiency and reduced organic loading. As a consequence of increasing the rate of the processes, the required capital investment also has been reduced significantly.

In many developing countries there is a need to improve the environment and to address the shortage of energy. In China and India, village communities are paying increasing attention to this need. Dairy cows are one simple accessible source of energy that many rural communities have. One hundred twenty-five dairy cows can produce 100 kWh.d-1 at 25% overall efficiency. The daily production of 100 kWh could satisfy a daily duty cycle of 6 hours at 100% output of a 9.3 kW engine, 6 hours at 40% output, and 12 hours at 20% output. This cycle is representative of the requirements in an agricultural community in the tropics where a typical household would require about 2 kWh per day.

Industrial country applications of anaerobic digestion are in three main areas: digestion of aerobic sewage treatment sludges at waste water treatment plants, treatment of industrial process effluent in breweries, distilleries, sugar processing, and pulp and paper mills, and in animal excreta treatment in concentrated animal feed operations. This last area offers the opportunity to manage not just carbon, but also the nutrients such as nitrogen, phosphorus, and potassium.

Population, Food, and Land

The daily nutritional requirements of an adult are 2,500 kcal per day. This input into the human machine is capable of producing as much as 1 kW in short bursts. To give this context, when sleeping, the human body runs at around 20 W. Starches and sugars provide more than half the caloric input; cereals provide the majority of caloric input that is gained from car-

> *"A deadly combination of solid fuel, inefficient stoves and poor ventilation triggers off a complex mixture of health-damaging pollutants in homes."*
>
> World Health Organization Statement, 2000

bohydrates. The remainder comes from vegetables, fruits, meats, and fish. The precise combination of food sources is a function of income, lifestyle, and culture.

The annual food energy demand is around 21 EJ for 6 billion people. The total quantity would be 1.4 Gt if it were all from grains. The world grain production is 1.9 Gt, of which wheat is 590 Mt and rice is 398 Mt. Most grains are consumed in the country of origin. Only about 12% of production (or 220 million tons) is traded, i.e. exported by the world's store-houses such as the United States, Australia, Latin America, and Europe and imported by other countries with low food production potential such as the highly urbanized Netherlands, or the populated desert regions. Grain stores stand at 17% of the annual production–a reserve of 60 to 80 days of production.

Unfortunately, food is not distributed equitably. About 800 million of the world's 6 billion people do not have enough to eat. There are 4.4 billion people living in developing countries and one-third of these live on less than a dollar a day. Poverty and marginalization of peoples creates chronic food insecurity in rural and predominantly agricultural societies.

The overall food supply situation is not ideal, but is considered satisfactory. It is still subject to climate fluctuation, natural disasters, and man-made situations such as wars, physical destruction, and population displacements. The Green Revolution and continuing innovations, such as the new hybrid rice crops in Southeast Asia, suggest that the food supply in general can keep up with the increasing population. Land itself is in short supply, and in general the future will consist of increasingly intense land cultivation to meet agricultural needs.

This pathway has already been followed in the United States. Corn now yields on average more than 10 times per hectare what it did in 1945. As a result, the U.S. now produces more corn than ever and uses less land to do it. Intensive villages such as IREF and Hacienda Flora (see case study #1) can also increase land productivity. But, for many crops in developing countries, the harvest yields are only a small fraction of the yields in industrialized agriculture in the OECD countries. Agricultural yields obtained on farms in developing countries can be a small fraction of yields obtained at national Agricultural Research and Extension farms.

Biotechnology

Recent discussions about advances in agriculture, such as genetically modified organisms (GMOs), have taken a disturbingly irrational turn. Response from industrialized nations, reflected in the term "Frankenfoods," may be entirely inappropriate in the face of rising population and world food demand. Rather than denying the technology's benefits, the GMO issue should be managed responsibly. Genome-based technologies are just one more step in a progression that has improved corn productivity by a factor of 8-10 in the U.S. since the 1930s.

Biotechnology provides promise to increase efficiency of food production. Table 1 summarizes ongoing biotechnology research to meet some of the needs of long-recognized developing countries.

The FAO's electronic forum on biotechnology and its conferences are bridging some of the information gaps (see (http://www.fao.org/biotech/forum.htm). They are providing information and hopefully helping to reach a consensus on an area of major importance in this century: biotechnology has the potential to help increase production and productivity in agriculture, forestry, and fisheries. It could lead to higher yields on marginal lands in countries that today cannot grow enough food to feed their citizens.

Genetic engineering has already helped reduce the transmission of human and animal diseases through new vaccines. Rice has been genetically engineered to contain pro-vitamin A (beta-carotene) and iron, which can improve the health of many low-income communities. Other biotechnological methods have led to organisms that improve food quality and consistency. Tissue culture has produced plants that are increasing crop yields by providing farmers with healthier planting material, materials that are virus free thus increasing crop yields by as much as 40% over "normal" plants. Genetic marker-assisted selection and DNA fingerprinting allow for faster and more targeted development of improved genotypes for all living species. The new techniques will enable scientists to recognize and target quantitative trait loci on chromosomes and thus increase the efficiency of

Table 1 - Needs of developing countries and the new biotechnologies

Basic Need	Potential Contribution of New biotechnologies	Dominent Research of Biotech Industry
Crop Production		
Conservation and improvement of diverse poor people´s crops emphasizing hardiness, nutrition and yield	Tissue culture technology could support conservation and breeding objectives	Rather than pest resistance the focus is on gene transfer for pesticide resistance, encapsulated embryos and yield improvement for major crops only.
Food Processing		
Key concerns are durability, nutrition, and cost. Product and production should be culturally and environmentally sensitive making the best use of local resources.	Improvement of traditional fermentation methods and development of new possibilities	Focus is on reducing or substituting raw materials and the factory production of agricultural products
Animal Husbandry		
Conserve diversity and broaden breeding efforts for foraging animals to develop healthier, more efficient livestock. Develop multi-purpose domesticates	Vaccines and diagnostics can support these efforts and embryo transfer can help preserve diversity	Attention is on complete control over fertility and reproduction to develop high yielding uniform, but highly vulnerable breeds and also on veterinarian packages and on use of livestock as bio-reactors for drugs.
Health Care		
Best way to improve health is to eliminate poverty. Following that preventive health care focusing on improved sanitation, nutrition and drinking water. Next, new vaccines for tropical diseases and AIDS.	Biotechnologies could help with monoclonal antibodies for water testing and gene technology for vaccine research and production	Emphasis is on diagnostics and clinical assays, help against infertility, production of hormones and drugs related to aging, cancer, AIDS, heart disease and organ transplants and gene therapy.

[i] Cary Fowler, The Laws of Life: Another Development and the New Biotechnologies (Uppsala, Sweden: Dab Hammarskjold Foundation, 1988).

breeding for some traditionally intractable agronomic problems such as drought resistance and improved root systems.

There are concerns about the potential risks posed by certain aspects of biotechnology. These risks fall into two basic categories: the effects on human and animal health and the environmental consequences. Continued development and management is needed to reduce the risks of transferring toxins from one life form to another, of creating new toxins, and of transferring allergenic compounds from one species to another resulting in unexpected allergic reactions. Risks to the environment include the possibility of out-crossing (mating between unrelated individuals of the same species). Out-crossing could lead to the development of more aggressive weeds or wild relatives with increased resistance to diseases or environmental stresses. The result would be an upsetting of the ecosystem balance.[10]

Land Base

The land base is clearly under population pressure. Urban expansion often takes place on good agricultural land and frequently diverts the water that was previously used for crop irrigation to urban uses. Irrigated lands are becoming saline and less productive in many areas. Here too a biomass and bioenergy strategy is becoming part of a multipurpose solution. In India, tree plantations have been established on abandoned saline soils to provide building materials, fuelwood, and rehabilitated soil for producing of fodder and vegetables. Examples of multipurpose biomass production and use in India are abundant. The M.S. Swaminathan Foundation sponsored village activities demonstrating intensive integrated farming systems that are now producing shrimp, bees, and a variety of crops, many more products than the rice and lentils that were cultivated in the past. The seven principles upon which these successes were built are: soil care, water harvesting, crop, pest, and energy management, postharvest care, market links, organization, and empowerment.

Biomass Technologies Empower the Poor to Improve their Lives

Three case studies exemplify how biomass technologies can empower the poor to improve their lives – create employment, increase the quality of their lives, and simultaneously improve their environment. All examples are based on improving the efficiency of use of biomass – this means that more energy per unit of mass is delivered and less pollution is emitted to the homes of the rural poor – where it poses significant health impacts to women and children. The higher the efficiency of the technologies to generate cooking energy from biomass, the less biomass is needed for this purpose, the fewer emissions released to an indoor environment.

The three cases will highlight:

1. An integrated system for biomass as a source of food, feed, energy, and independence in comparison to imported energy and products.
2. A system for integrating residues from agricultural development to produce energy both in a small and larger scale.
3. An integrated system for the use of various renewable resources for food, products, energy, and income for villagers; an example of a joint venture that created a renewable energy service company; and a possible model for the future.

Case Study 1. Strategies for Increasing Local Self-Reliance – Flora Communite Agro-Ecological Village in the Philippines

Much of the land base in the sugarcane-growing regions of Negros Occidental, Philippines, is maintained in intensively managed monoculture plantations. Major economic and environmental problems have resulted from this method of rural development. Negros is still one of the areas of highest concentration of poor people in the Philippines. In 1995, the Philippine Government initiated the Comprehensive Agrarian Reform Program designed to meet rural residents' economic and social needs by reducing dependence on food imports and environmental damage caused by traditional farming techniques. An 87-hectare estate was awarded to 76 hacienda workers and their families. It is called the Flora Communite. A case study, undertaken by Resource Efficient Agricultural Production-Canada, the University of the Philippines at Los Banos, MASIPAG, a Philippine farmer/scientist partnership organization, and recently with the involvement of the U.S. Agency for International Development/National Renewable Energy Lab is examining the transition of a large sugarcane plantation to a diversified, self-supporting, sustainable, agricultural village. The Flora Communite is on its way to becoming an "agro-ecological village" through the use of organic-based farming practices – with both low- and high-tech solutions and renewable energy systems.

Transitioning from Traditional Practices to an Agro-Ecological Village

Transitioning from traditional practices to an agro-ecological village involves improving the quality of life and increasing opportunities for economic development by:

- Reducing dependence on food imports by on-site production of seasonal vegetables, rice, corn, root crops, fruit, fish, and eggs
- Replacing most tractor and fossil fuel with carabaos (water buffaloes) for soil tillage and hauling
- Replacing chemical fertilizers with nitrogen-fixing legumes and azolla (a floating aquatic plant) planted with rice

- Cycling minerals through the use of a "mudpress"(a by-product of sug-arcane processing), rice hull ash, carabao dung and preventing soil erosion with straw field composting and thrash farming of sugar cane
- Replacing herbicides with mechanical weeding devices, crop rota-tion, mulching, and good soil fertility management
- Replacing insecticides and fungicides with biological control strate-gies, balanced fertility, and resistant cultivars
- Improving agricultural plants and maintaining community seed banking instead of buying hybrid seeds
- Developing marketing strategies designed to maximize self-reliance and minimize dependence on imports; infrastructure improvements and investments will be needed
- Reducing greenhouse gas emissions through:
- Use of solar or biomass energy instead of fossil fuels for crop drying
- Use of more efficient irrigation techniques, such as water catchment ponds and windmills instead of gasoline/diesel-powered pumps
- Use of farm-derived biofuels, including rice hull cookers and efficient wood stoves instead of liquid propane gas fuel stoves or open-fire cooking; substantially reduces kerosene for fire-starter of wet wood since rice hull is a dry fuel
- Produce electricity from renewable sources, such as solar and micro-hydro instead of fossil fuel-based sources
- Build houses with bamboo, farm-derived wood, and rammed earth instead of cement blocks

Current Status of the Community

After a long struggle to gain land ownership, the Flora Communite is now making progress toward greater self-sufficiency and community improvement.

Approximately 90% of the community's energy requirements in the fields are now provided through animal power. After harvest, rice straw is returned to the soil to decompose, completely eliminating the practice of burning it in the field. Field composting of crop residues returns nutrients to the soil, minimizing the use of chemical fertilizers. A mobile rice mill reduces time and cost of transport and allows rice hulls to remain in the community for fuel and nutrient cycling. In 1999, the Lo-Trau rice hull cook stove was introduced for household use, minimizing use of firewood, charcoal, kerosene, and propane. Appropriate technology decreased cook-ing time.

The community has steadily reduced its need to import food sources by replacing commercial sugarcane production with food crops production. Crops now produced in addition to sugarcane are glutinous and white grain corn, rice, eggplant, squash, sweet corn, radish, peanuts, bush sitao, mungbeans, sweet potato, gabi, and cassava. Increased production of fish, poultry and eggs has reduced the need to purchase these items from the market. *This case study indicates that the stability of a sound ecological agricultural system is achieved through multiple means of supplying important functions. The shift from conventional farming practices to agro-ecological systems is a promising approach to global poverty alleviation and greenhouse gas emissions reduction.*[10]

Case 2. Bioenergy Technology and Use in Rural China

Up to 70% of China's 1.26 billion people live in rural areas. As rural incomes have steadily increased, villagers have had the means to replace their use of natural sources of cooking fuel (wood and straw and stalks from cereals and grains) with fossil fuels (kerosene, coal, and liquid petroleum gases – LPG). Extensive air pollution has resulted from both in-field burning of crop residues and combustion of fossil fuels. China's Ministry of Agriculture and the U. S. Department of Energy have sought to develop technologies to produce fuel and electricity from biomass instead of from fossil fuels. The successful development and deployment of renewable energy systems in rural areas will increase rural incomes, reduce dependence on fossil fuels, and reduce greenhouse gas emissions.

Two technologies currently under development in China are biogas production from the effluent from dairy operations, and gasification of straws and stalks from rice, wheat, and maize.

Biogas Production

Formerly, the effluent from dairy operations was discharged directly to adjacent fields to allow natural biodegradation and nutrient cycling processes to occur. As China's demand for meat and milk increases, expanded dairy operations have overwhelmed the land's ability to deal with higher amounts of nutrients. In 1997, for example, a dairy farm in the Shanghai Province expanded its operation to three thousand cows, which produce 30,000 tons of manure per year. Releasing the effluents to the fields without treatment resulted in very high organic and bacterial pollution levels in the river serving the province.

To deal with organic wastes from increasing urbanization and intensification of chicken, pork, beef, and milk production, over 600 medium- and large-scale biogas treatment facilities using anaerobic digestion technology are currently in use.   The biogas treatment process involves four main steps:

- Pre-treatment of the fermentable materials in which bedding straw is separated from dung and returned to the field after composting. The dung is passed to an open top acidic pre-treatment facility where the biodegradation of cellulose and hemi-cellulose occurs. Non-solubles float to the top as scum and are removed. The remaining acidic slurry is pumped into anaerobic digestors for fermentation.
- The remaining slurry is stored for secondary treatment.
- After fermentation, the product gas is purified and metered to consumers. Secondary treatment of digested slurry prevents pollution.
- Treated slurry is discharged to adjacent fields.

Biogas composition is 50-60% methane, approximately 50% carbon dioxide, with traces of ammonia and hydrogen sulfide. Heating value is just over half that of natural gas, at 25mJ/m. Using this technology, 30,000 tons of manure per year supply over 3,000 households and several hotels with a source of clean-burning, renewable gas.

Straw Gasification

China grows rice, wheat, and maize that produce approximately 600 million tons of dried straw and stalks. Most of this fiber is used as animal fodder, paper production, and nutrient cycling. The remainder, nearly 200 million tons, is burned in fields. Straw contains sulfur, nitrogen, and carbon, which pollute the air and emit greenhouse gases when burned. Straw gasifiers, through the use of biomass pyrolysis gasification technology, have enabled high-quality utilization of a low-quality material to improve the daily lives of rural Chinese residents and offset use of fossil fuels.

In a typical gasifier, straw particles that have been chopped to 15-20 cm in length and dried to 20% moisture content, are fed into a combustion chamber and ignited. Product gases, tar, and ash are extracted from the gasifier by blowers that send the gas to storage after cooling and purification. The carbon and hydrogen present in the straw are converted to methane, carbon monoxide, hydrogen, carbon dioxide, and water vapor in the product gas.

Gasifiers can produce clean-burning gas from corn stalks and cobs, wheat straw, bean shells, and bark and wood shavings. Approximately 3 kg of straw can produce enough gas for daily household needs. Gasification of 100,000 tons of straw can save 200,000 tons of coal. The gas can be used directly for cooking energy, some gas can be used for heating homes in the cold regions like Jilin, and excess gas can generate electricity using engines for the village and for export to the grid or other villages.

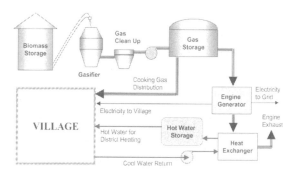

More information on bioenergy technology and utilization can be found at the following sites:

http://www.nrel.gov/international/china/pdfs/re_forum/biopower_hydropower_technologies.pdf

http://www.nrel.gov/international/china/re_forum.html

http://www.nrel.gov/international/china/pdfs/renewable_energy_markets_in_china.pdf

Case 3. Bioenergy and Other Products in Rural Philippines – a New Renewable Energy Service Company (RESCO)

Community Power Corporation (CPC)[11] provides an example of a small business company with powerful partners developing creative solutions for rural communities. In a joint partnership with Shell Renewables, the 150 household village of Alaminos on the island of Panay in the Philippines is now able to use coconuts for food purposes and productively use the residues through gasification. The gas is burned to make heat for processing the coconuts and also to make electricity for the village. This electricity is used not only for the commercial activity but also to recharge the batteries of the many photovoltaic systems that generate electricity for the individual homes.

CPC's activities include product design, equipment procurement and supply, product development, tariff design, revenue collection design, equipment installation, training customers & staff, and monitoring and analysis. Shell Renewables' activities include project financing, secure licenses/approvals, legal dealings, establishing the local company, site management, equipment operation, maintenance, revenue collection, data collection, and project replication.

Technology improvements in all three examples enable the poor to increase their quality of life:

- They will spend significantly less time gathering biomass for cooking.
- They will prepare food faster with better quality cookstoves and increase indoor air quality because of the higher efficiency of the stove or gasification system.

An illustration of how these technologies improve the minimum needs is shown in the figure below.

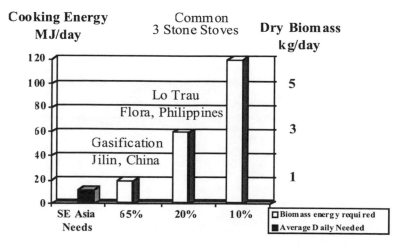

EFFICIENCY OF COOK STOVE OR GASIFIER USED TO GENERATE COOKING ENERGY

Why Replicate These and Other Successful Projects?

These projects have the potential to increase local employment and productively use residue resources from agriculture that otherwise could create significant environmental problems. For instance, in the period of 1980-1990, the United States developed a biomass power industry primarily using clean wood residues from urban areas, residues from forest products manufacturing, and agriculture residues. In the process of harnessing 7,000 MW of electricity, 66,000 jobs were created, and U.S.$15 billion was invested, generating a net U.S.$2 billion annual income industry. Each year, this biopower prevents the emission of 7.2 million tons of carbon. It also diverts biomass from the landfills, thus increasing their lifetime.

Assuming a similar proportion of jobs is created in developing countries, nearly 10 jobs would be created per MW of capacity. Jobs would also be created in the development of the infrastructure for electricity, home heating, and cooking gas. The construction of these various facilities would also generate additional jobs for a short period of time (year). In addition, jobs can be created through the development of local manufacturing capability. Since these projects are small (0.02-1 MW), the real impact is only felt if they are replicated widely.

How to Replicate These and Other Successful Projects

Bundling projects or aggregating customers is needed because the cost of projects is high for multilateral donors. This bundling can facilitate dissemination and large-scale deployment of these technologies. There are still difficulties in identifying multiple projects in a single country. Therefore, help in project identification and definition is needed. For instance, 10 additional projects replicating the Alaminos project have been identified in the Philippines. Bundling all ten would save significant resources and increase the efficiency of their deployment and operations.

Adopt a Stove

A new model is emerging of how to provide technology that is adapted to the developing countries in a highly efficient manner. CPC (http://www.gocpc.com/) has developed a TurboStoveTM, based on a small-scale high efficiency gasification closed system coupled with a combustion system with twice the efficiency of the Lo Trau cooker.[12] CPC created a not-for-profit company called Productive Rural Enterprises to adapt the TurboStove concept to specific developing countries, according to their customs and cooking needs. Shell Foundation is currently sponsoring a Productive Rural Enterprises' project to create manufacturing capability for locally adapted high-efficiency stoves designed with the help of the community. The first phase includes four countries. Substantially more partners are needed to increase the scope of these activities to impact an increasing fraction of the 2 billion people dependent on biomass for their cooking energy needs.

Just imagine that an investment of about $100,000 creates a stove adapted to a community and the manufacturing capacity to supply about 1000 households per year. This can be replicated hundreds or thousands of times. The process of developing the stoves for a particular community addresses two problems simultaneously. First, the stove will be used because of community involvement in its development. Second, a permanent manufacturing capacity is created that can service thousands of households.

If the world community were to rapidly develop 100,000 manufacturing centers throughout the world, they could replace low efficiency cookstoves, increase rural employment, develop entrepreneurs, and solve an environmental problem that is becoming widely recognized. Assuming that a $100,000 creates a center, then $10-50 million could significantly help the world's 2 billion poor improve their quality of life and seed economic development in the rural areas, balancing opportunities for rural and urban areas.

What the new model needs is replication. Imagine if private sponsors, multiple foundations, and governments were to collaboratively sponsor such a development. Imagine if a few private sponsors around the world were to "ADOPT A VILLAGE" to create a manufacturing center for high efficiency cookstoves. Imagine if these sponsors shared the development information, both about the costs and training. The rate of development would be greatly accelerated since similar customs apply to many of the villages in a given watershed, country, or region. Tremendous savings opportunities exist for this cooperative learning.

An "ADOPT A VILLAGE" program could become a solution to a serious world problem. It could be made by multiple sponsors selecting a mechanism for combined action – a low overhead mechanism with extensive data sharing and a "training the trainers" capability. Mobilizing the existing infrastructure of many non-governmental organizations already operating in several countries could rapidly create a significant rural manufacturing capacity in stoves. Stoves are just a beginning!

We hope that The Aspen Institute and the participants in its global poverty conference can help provide a forum for discussions of non-governmental organizations and other groups to further elaborate and develop the "ADOPT A VILLAGE" concept. The concept has its origins in discussions with attendees at the Aspen Institute 50th anniversary meeting, who wanted to know how they could contribute, individually, to getting high efficiency cookstoves adopted by developing countries. It was those discussions and subsequent dialogue with poverty conference collegues that furthered this concept.

Acknowledgments: Robb Walt from Community Power Corporation contributed significantly to the development of the ADOPT A VILLAGE program concept. The assistance of Cheryl Jurich is greatly appreciated. We also acknowledge the long-term support and encouragement of our colleagues in the U.S. Department of Energy through the Office of Energy Efficiency and Renewable Energy who have made it possible for NREL to contribute to this important area.

ENDNOTES

1. UNDP, Human Development Report, New York, 1994.

2. Science and Technology for Poverty Alleviation and Social Development in the American Hemisphere, Available at,
<http://www.unesco.org.uy/ciencias-basicas/libroscsbs/ventura/frame.html>

3. Social work following the implementation of U.S. Department of Energy and Brazilian Ministry of Mines and Energy rural electrification in specific cities of the states of Ceara and Pernambuco using two models. Private communication to Helena Chum (1997).

4. See, for instance, UNDP China activities at the web site:
http://www.edu.cn/undp/ccp/cp4/ccf/themes.htm

5. See, for instance, Sustainable Communities by the U.S. President's Council for Sustainable Development, 1997, http://www.whitehouse.gov/PCSD/Publications/suscomm/ind_suscom.html; International Centre for Sustainable Cities (Canada) at http://www.icsc.ca/; European Sustainable Cities Project at http://euronet.uwe.ac.uk/euro-sustcit/project.htm; Sustainable Cities program of the UNDP http://www.undp.org/un/habitat/scp/; International Council for Local Environmental Initiatives (ICLEI), association of 300 local governments dedicated to the prevention and solution of local, regional, and global environmental problems through local action at http://www.iclei.org/.

6. See, for instance, Rural and Small Towns Programme, Canada, at http://www.mta.ca/rstp/rstpmain.html; National Rural Development Partnership in the U.S. at http://www.rurdev.usda.gov/nrdp/; Sustainable Agricultural and Rural Development (Guyana) at http://www.sardguyana.org/; Appropriate Technology Transfer for Rural Areas at http://www.attra.org/

7. Village Earth, The Consortium for Sustainable Village-based Development at http://www.villageearth.org/

8. Examples of references, many of them available electronically through http://www.nrel.gov/villagepower/program/program.html include: Touryan, J. O. V.; Touryan, K. J. (1999). Renewable Energy for Sustainable Rural Village Power. 11 pp.; NICH Report No. CP-720-26871; Village Power '98: Scaling Up Electricity Access for Sustainable Rural Development (CD-ROM). Proceedings of the Village Power '98 Conference, 6-8 October 1998, Washington, DC. (1999). ; NICH Report No. CP-500-26264; Flowers, L. (1998). Lessons Learned - NREL Village Power Program. 6 pp.; NICH Report No. CP-500-24938; Jimenez, A. C.; Olson, K. (1998). Energia Renovable para Centros de Salud Rurales. 52 pp.; NICH Report No. BK-500-26224; Taylor, R. (1998). Lessons Learned from the NREL Village Power Program. 5 pp.; NICH Report No. CP-210-25032; Burch, J.; Thomas, K. E. (1998). Overview of Water Disinfection in Developing Countries and the Potential for Solar Thermal Water Pasteurization. 114 pp.; NICH Report No. TP-550-23110; Niewoehner, J.; Larson, R.; Azrag, E.; Hailu, T.; Horner, J.; VanArsdale, P. (1997). Opportunities for Renewable Energy Technologies in Developing Country Villages. 72 pp.; NICH Report No.

SR-430-22359; Cardinal, J.; Flowers, L.; Taylor, R.; Weingart, J. (1997). Proceedings of Village Power '97, 14-15 April 1997, Arlington, Virginia. Golden, CO: National Renewable Energy Laboratory; 521 pp.; NICH Report No. CP-440-23409; Corbus, D.; Bergey, M. (1997). Costa de Cocos 11-kW Wind-Diesel Hybrid Power System. 12 pp.; NICH Report No. CP-440-23296; Castedo, S.; Corbus, D.; Flowers, L.; Holz, R.; Lew, D.; McAllister, A. (1996). Wind Hybrid Systems Applications for Rural Electrification: The Case Study of Chile. Zervos, A.; Ehmann, H.; Helm, P., eds. Proceedings of the 1996 European Union Wind Energy International Conference, 20-24 May 1996, Goteborg, Sweden. United Kingdom: H. S. Stephens and Associates; pp. 301-304; NICH Report No. 26182.

9. Nasir El Bassam is with the German Federal Agricultural Research Ministry's Institution of Crop Science in Braunschweig.

10. See, for instance, the statement on biotechnology by the Food and Agriculture Organization of the United Nations, http://www.fao.org/biotech/state.htm.

11. Contact: Roger Samson and Lindsey Mulkins. Resource Efficient Agricultural Production-Canada, REAP@Interlink.net, www.reap.ca; Louie Amongo and Emmanuel Yap. MASIPAG, masipag@mozcom.com; Teodoro Mendoza. University of the Philippines Los Banos, Department of Agronomy, TCM@mudspring.uplb.edu.ph

12. Contact: Art Lilley artsolar@gocpc.com or Robb Walt rwalt@gocpc.com at Community Power Corporation, 8420 S. Continental Divide Road, Suite #100, Littleton, CO 80127; see http://www.gocpc.com/; http://www.rsvp.nrel.gov/vpconference/Wrural/lilley.pdf.

The authors can be reached at the National Renewable Energy Laboratory: Ralph_Overend@nrel.gov and Helena_Chum@nrel.gov.

Broadband Via Satellite Reaches Everywhere*

By Santiago Ontañón**
August 19, 2000

I am going to talk about high-performance satellite broadband as a contribution to poverty alleviation. As many of you know, satellites have been providing commercial communications to remote places for about 30 or 40 years. The emerging use of satellites to deliver Internet Protocol (IP) has brought new life to satellites, as data transmission efficiencies and lower costs have been achieved in the last 18 months. This has created connectivity and new opportunities in areas formerly cut off from information technology. It is becoming very simple to broadcast the Internet to remote places. The challenge now is to bring those remote places to the Internet so they can contribute to the richness of the Internet and use it for interactive applications, such as e-commerce, e-mail, or telephone conversations using voice-over IP.

The Technology

Figure 1 gives an overview of the basic architecture of a broadband satellite system. A number of companies are using and developing this type of technology. Some companies, like Tachyon, Inc., are developing technology from the ground up; and others are adapting old satellite technology to work in the Internet environment. There are two major elements in the architecture. One is the access point where enterprise users access the Internet through a small satellite dish that allows for connections both ways—from user to the Internet and the Internet to the user—through the satellite, to a central location close to the fiber infrastructure. As many of you are aware, there is a lot of fiber being built around the world. However, the fiber only reaches the major cities of the world. With the broadband satellite solution, everyone within the satellite footprint benefits from the fiber infrastructure. This very simple solution looks like a typical satellite network, but it is interesting to note the speed of the link and that it can go both ways. For a single user, these networks can achieve up to 30 megabits

---

*   Remarks delivered at the Aspen Institute International Peace, Security & Prosperity Program conference on *"Alleviating Global Povery: Technology for Economic & Social Uplift,"* in Aspen, Colorado, August 18-20, 2000.

** Santiago Ontañón is former Vice President, Corporate Development, Tachyon, Inc.

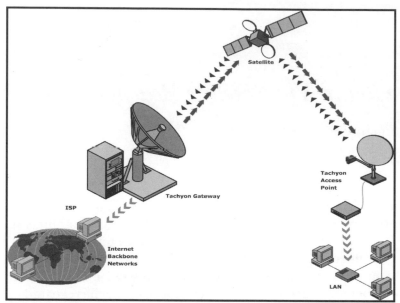

Figure 1. Basic System Architecture © Tachyon, Inc.

per second from the Internet to the user and about 256 to 512 kilobits per second on the return channel.

The outdoor units are pointed to the satellite and are connected to an indoor unit. From there, a simple cable (standard RJ45) plugs into the indoor unit to connect the entire local area network. Companies are trying to make the technology and the interface with technology as simple as possible.

I would like to emphasize why the Internet currently is so slow in rural places. As Figure 2 shows, typically enterprise users, such as schools, connect to the Internet through a number of points of presence (POPs). They are connected to their local Internet Service Provider (ISP), which is connected to the regional ISP, connected to a national ISP, and finally connected to a Tier 1 ISP somewhere in the United States. With satellite technology one goes directly into the heart of the backbone, increasing the speed of the link and also going closer to where the content is hosted.

Current systems use geo-stationary satellites orbiting the earth around the equator to reach places. They cannot cover the poles, but most of the population of the world can be covered. Many operators are not employing their own satellites. Some use other people's satellites that, in general, have footprints that cover whole regions around the globe. Figure 3 depicts several typical geo-stationary footprints.

Today companies are operating in North America and Europe. By the end of next year, some will be extending out into the Americas, Asia, the Middle East, and Australia. Depending on the financing conditions, some companies may venture into other areas, such as Africa, India, and South East Asia.

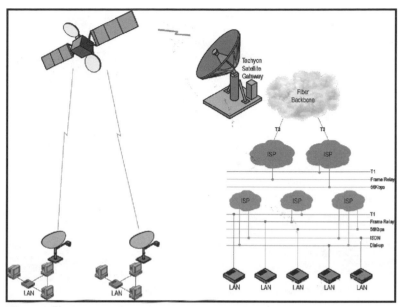

Figure 2. Congestion bypass. © Tachyon, Inc.

High-speed fiber is aggressively being deployed around the globe. Figure 4 exemplifies a state of the art network being deployed in South America, where there are at least three major companies planning to provide access to these types of links. But, as you can see, these fiber networks only reach the major cities in the region.

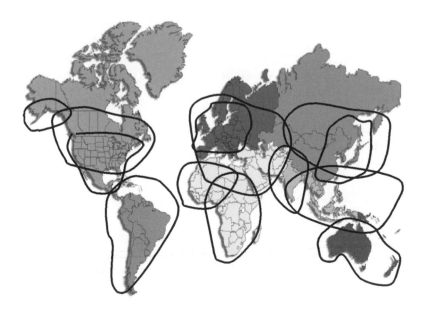

Figure 3. Global footprints © Tachyon, Inc.

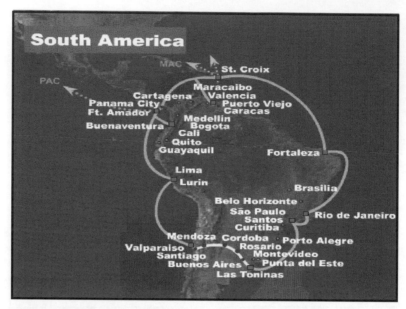

Figure 4. Regional fiber ring. © Global Crossing

With a satellite footprint it is possible to take every single square inch of South America into the high performance-high speed fiber. Users could be connected as if they were in downtown São Paulo or downtown Buenos Aires. The only thing one needs to use satellite broadband is to be able to see the sky. The installation and deployment of satellite broadband users is simple and inexpensive.

What you see in Figures 5 is a fisherman's restaurant. The owner rented some space in his parking lot to put up the antenna and give a demonstration. It is quite interesting to note the infrastructure he had. He had electricity that appeared to be "taken" directly from the electricity post. Using his parking lot, his electricity, and a shack to house the indoor unit, he had one of the fastest connections to the Internet in the whole continent. The speed of adoption was comparable to the connection. These two guys had never been to the Internet. Unfortunately this photograph shows them with their hands off, but within five minutes they had quickly mastered the basic rules of surfing the Internet, and were quite active moving the laptop's pointing device and in surfing the Internet.

Costs Go Down

What about the trends that we are seeing in terms of where technology is leading us? In terms of price, technology is going to drive down the cost of this type of equipment.

Today, the equipment for enterprise grade broadband via satellite sells for less than US$6,000 in the United States. The user then has to pay a monthly rent for the service. The price around the world varies because

Figure 5. Broadband pioneers in Brazil

of tariffs and local taxes, but in general, we are seeing that prices will go down significantly. The gap between the cost in the United States and in the developing nations, for example, is also going to narrow. In terms of the price of the bandwidth, or the monthly cost, it is also being driven down by smart technology, compression, and more powerful satellites. In terms of coverage, it is interesting to look at the satellite industry starting from the old Intelsat system, which tried to cover enormous regions with a single satellite footprint. Currently, the trend is to cover smaller regions.

In terms of business models, today there are satellite solutions in Latin America that take advantage of the geographical proximity of that region to the United States. These satellite connections bypass the local infrastructure and telephone. The profits are also bypassed into the United States. With regional fiber rings and regional footprints, one can take the whole continent of South America into the fiber-rich main cities. I believe that fiber is the best way to connect two distant known points on the planet, e.g., connecting any city on the continent of South America to the United States Internet backbone.

Obstacles

We are seeing that the next generation of satellite systems is facing many problems in financing. With the shutdown of Iridium, the low-earth-orbit-satellite phone system, there has been much doubt about the ability to use this type of spacecraft for broadband Internet. The problem for the developing world goes further as these sophisticated multi-billion dollar projects are targeted to serve only the most populated areas of the developed world. Some of these systems turn off their satellites when they are flying over the less developed nations.

When satellite systems do cover less developed areas, they still face archaic regulatory regimes that protect the interests of the local telephone monopolies. Deregulation is very important for this technology to work. You can immediately light a whole region; but, the problem lies in obtaining permission in every country from each government to provide services.

In conclusion, today the technology is available to provide broadband Internet connections to everyone on the planet. If investment and regulatory barriers are overcome, the rewards can be enormous. Researchers at universities around the world have studied the effects of leapfrogging into broadband Internet connections and the significant benefits that this brings to education, medicine, community building, the environment, etc. Most of these studies have been conducted in fairly connected areas of the world. One can only imagine that more remote locations will benefit significantly too as the Information Revolution reaches them and opens new prospects for progress.

List of Conference Participants

CONFERENCE CHAIRMAN

José María Figueres
    Managing Director, World Economic Forum; former President of Costa Rica; Founder, The Foundation for Sustainable Development (Costa Rica)

MODERATOR

Shashi Tharoor
    Director of Communications and Special Projects, Office of the UN Secretary General, The United Nations; World Economic Forum Global Leader for Tomorrow

PARTICIPANTS

Shem Arungu–Olende
    Consultant in Science and Technology and Software Development; former staff member, United Nations

Jacques Attali
    President, PlaNet Finance (France); President, Attali & Associés; former President, European Bank for Reconstruction and Development (EBRD)

Hattie Babbitt
    Deputy Administrator, U.S. Agency for International Development; former U.S. Permanent Representative to the Organization of American States

Prince Bandar bin Sultan
    Ambassador of the Kingdom of Saudi Arabia to the United States

Carlos Braga
    Program Manager, Information for Development (InfoDev), The World Bank

Nayan Chanda
    Editor-at-Large, *Far Eastern Economic Review*

Helena Chum
    Director of the Bioenergy Systems Center, National Renewable Energy Laboratory (USA)

Nancy Bearg Dyke
    Director, International Peace, Security & Prosperity Program, The Aspen Institute; Conference Director

Fan Gang	Director, National Economic Research Institute, China Reform Foundation; World Economic Forum Global Leader for Tomorrow
Mircea Geoana	Ambassador of Romania to the United States
Bill Joy	Co-Founder and Chief Scientist, Sun Microsystems, Inc.
Princeton Lyman	Executive Director, Global Interdependence Initiative, The Aspen Institute; former U.S. Ambassador to Nigeria and South Africa
Andrew Maguire	CEO, EnterpriseWorks Worldwide; former U.S. Representative
Joseph Nye	Don K. Price Professor of Public Policy and Dean of the Kennedy School of Government, Harvard University
Santiago Ontañón	Former Vice President, Corporate Development, Tachyon, Inc.
Olara Otunnu	Under-Secretary-General, The United Nations; Special Representative of the Secretary General for Children and Armed Conflict
Hisashi Owada	President, Japan Institute of International Affairs; former Permanent Representative of Japan to the United Nations
Iqbal Quadir	Co-Founder of GrameenPhone (Bangladesh); World Economic Forum Global Leader for Tomorrow
Theo Sommer	Editor-at-Large, *Die Zeit* (Germany); Boardmember, Deutsche Welthungerhilfe
Edith Ssempala	Ambassador of Uganda to the United States
Timothy Wirth	Director and President, United Nations Foundation; former U.S. Undersecretary of State for Global Affairs; former U.S. Senator and Representative

STAFF

Nancy Bearg Dyke	Conference Director, International Peace, Security & Prosperity Program, The Aspen Institute
Marilyn Crane	Program Assistant for the conference, International Peace, Security & Prosperity Program, The Aspen Institute
Kevin Morrison	Conference Rapporteur; Fellow, Overseas Development Council
Stephanie Wethington	Program Assistant for the report, International Peace, Security & Prosperity Program, The Aspen Institute

Conference Agenda

FRIDAY, AUGUST 18, 2000
4:00-6:00 PM, **Keynote Address and Session I**

WHERE DOES TECHNOLOGY FIT IN A POVERTY REDUCTION STRATEGY?
- **Opening remarks by Conference Moderator, Shashi Tharoor**
- **Keynote address by Conference Chairman, José María Figueres**
- **Remarks by Bill Joy and Iqbal Quadir, followed by discussion**
  –What is the role of technology in economic and social development of poor countries and people?
  –Should technology be a central focus of developing country policy makers, or should it be viewed as complementary to their other efforts?
  –How can countries evaluate when they need to go "high-tech" as opposed to "low-tech?"
  –Is there a different role for technology in fighting poverty in low-income countries than in middle-income countries (or even high-income countries)?
  –What are the major ethical, social, cultural, and governance dilemmas centered around technology to alleviate poverty?
  –Whose responsibility is it to ensure that appropriate technological solutions reach the poor?
  –What broad lessons have been learned previously about introducing technology into development?

SATURDAY, AUGUST 19, 2000
8:30-10:15 AM, **Session II**

TECHNOLOGY TO EMPOWER THE POOR TO IMPROVE THEIR LIVES
- **Remarks by Edith Ssempala and Helena Chum, followed by discussion**
  –How can technology be used by poor people to improve their lives and surroundings?
  –What can be learned from past experiences, in fields such as renewable energy, about how technology can complement efforts to address basic needs and reduce suffering—such as through basic education, clean water, disease prevention, and food security?
  –What is necessary (such as policies or new research) to give poor people access to such technology in a sustainable way?
  –Are there effective products and techniques available now that should receive more emphasis and be made more widely available?

<u>10:30 AM-12:00 PM, **Session III**</u>

TECHNOLOGY, POOR PEOPLE, AND JOB CREATION
- **Remarks by Jacques Attali and Santiago Ontañón, followed by discussion**
  —To what extent can technology change the economic dynamics within a country to jumpstart development, such as by creating pockets of high-tech activity or enhancing other projects that broadly encourage economic activity and provide job opportunities?

  —Is this change possible even in countries with poor economic policy?

  —What is needed in terms of policy to provide the necessary technology to those who need it?

1:00 - 3:30 PM, **Opening Session of the Aspen Institute 50th Anniversary Symposium on** *"Globalization and the Human Condition"*
  - **Panel Discussion: Understanding Globalization, moderated by David Gergen**

6:30 - 7:15 PM, **50th Anniversary Symposium Speech by James D. Wolfensohn, "Making Globalization Work for the Poor"**

SUNDAY, AUGUST 20, 2000

<u>8:30 -11:45 AM, **Session IV**</u>

DEVISING A STRATEGY THAT HARNESSES TECHNOLOGY FOR POVERTY ALLEVIATION
- **Discussion**
  —Looking at what we have discussed, how does technology fit into an international strategy for poverty reduction?

  —What are the respective roles of governments, the private sector, NGOs, academia, and poor people themselves in maximizing the benefits of technology for poor people?

  —Specifically, what is the role of the international donor community and the international private sector?

  —What incentives need to be created in order to ensure that technology is transferred to where it is most needed?
- **Conclusions and recommendations**

Selected Readings and Internet Links

General Resources on Poverty Trends and Poverty Reduction

The Aspen Institute International Peace, Security & Prosperity Conference Reports
— *Alleviating Global Poverty: Technology for Economic and Social Uplift.* (Washington, D.C.: The Aspen Institute. 2001) Available at: <http://www.aspeninst.org/ipsp>
— *The International Poverty Gap: Investing in People and Technology to Build Sustainable Pathways Out.* (Washington, D.C.: The Aspen Institute. 2000.) Available at <http://www.aspeninst.org/ipsp>
— *Persistent Poverty In Developing Countries: Determining the Causes and Closing the Gaps.* Washington, D.C.: The Aspen Institute. 1998, Available at <http://aspeninstitute.org/ipsp/ipsp_publications.html>

Department for International Development, United Kingdom
— "Eliminating World Poverty: Making Globalisation Work for the Poor." White Paper on International Development. Available at <http://62.189.42.51>
— "Halving World Poverty by 2015: Economic Growth, Equity and Security." Available at <http://www.dfid.gov.uk/public/what/strategy_papers/target_strategy.html>

G8 Summit Okinawa, Japan, 23 July 2000.
— "G8 Communiqué, Okinawa, 2000." Available at <http://www.library.utoronto.ca/g7/summit/ 2000okinawa/finalcom.htm>
— "Okinawa Charter on Global Information Society." Available at <http://www.library.utoronto.ca/g7/summit/2000okinawa/gis.htm> and <http://www.g8kyushu-okinawa.go.jp/e/documents/it1.html>

— "Japan's Comprehensive Co-operation Package to Address the International Digital Divide." Available at: <http://www.g8kyushu-okinawa.go.jp/e/theme/it.html>

Organization for Economic Co-operation and Development
— Development Assistance Committee. "Development Cooperation: 2000 Report." *DAC Journal* 2001 2(1).
— Development Assistance Committee. "Development Cooperation: 1999 Report." *DAC Journal* 2000 1(1).
— "Technology, Productivity and Job Creation: Best Policy Practices, Highlights." 1998. Available at http://www.oecd.org/dsti/sti/prod/highlite.pdf>

United Nations

United Nations Development Programme. *Human Development Report.* New
    York: Oxford University Press. 1999. Available at
    <http://www.undp.org/hdro/99.htm>
  — "Ethics and Technology – A Luxury Concern?" p. 72.
  — "The Need to Reshape Technology's Path." pp. 72-76.
  — "Human Development Index." pp.157-160.
  — "Human Poverty in Developing Countries." pp. 169-171.
  — "Human Poverty in OECD, Eastern Europe and the CIS." pp. 172-173.
  — "Access to Information Flows." pp. 198-201.
United Nations Development Programme. *Human Development Report.*
    New York: Oxford University Press. 2000.
        Available at < http://www.undp.org/hdro/HDR2000.html>
United Nations Educational, Scientific and Cultural Organization. *World
    Culture Report 2000.* 2000. Available at
    <http://www.unesco.org/culture/worldreport/index.html>

World Bank

—Paul Collier and Anke Hoeffler, "Aid, Policy and Peace."
Available at
<http://www.worldbank.org/research/conflict/papers/aidpolicy.pdf>
—Paul Collier and Anke Hoeffler, "On Economic Causes of Civil War."
Available at
<http://www.worldbank.org/research/conflict/papers/cw-cause.pdf>
—Paul Collier and David Dollar, "Aid Allocation and Poverty Reduction."
Available at
<http://www.worldbank.org/aid/background/bg98_allocation_full.htm>
—David Dollar and Lant Pritchett, "Assessing Aid."
Available at <http://www.worldbank.org/aid/pdfs/front.pdf>
—World Bank. *World Development Report 1999/2000: Entering the 21st
Century.* Washington, D.C.: World Bank and Oxford University
Press.1999.
— World Bank. *World Development Report 2000/2001: Attacking Poverty.*
Washington, D.C.: World Bank and Oxford University Press. 2000.
–World Bank. *World Development Indicators.* Washington, D.C.:
World Bank. 2000.
—World Bank. *World Global Development Finance 2001: Building
Coalitions for Effective Development Finance* (Washington, D.C.: World
Bank, 2000).
— World Bank. Comprehensive Development Framework. Available at
<http://www.worldbank.org/cdf/>

Information on Specific Projects

The African Virtual University
    <http://www.avu.org>
Business Partners for Development (BPD)
    <http://www.bpdweb.org/projects.htm>
EnterpriseWorks

<http://www.enterpriseworks.org>
Global Development Gateway
<http://www.worldbank.org/gateway>
Greenstar
<http://www.greenstar.org>
International Campaign to Ban Landmines
<http://www.icbl.org>
Little Intelligent Communities Project (LINCOS)
<http://www.media.mit.edu/unwired/>
PCS Computer Academy
<http://pcsindia.com/home.html>
PlaNet Finance: Fighting Poverty through the Internet
<http://www.planetfinance.org>
Peoplink
<http://peoplink.org>
"Rural Water Supply: Simple Technology, Big Benefits for the Poor."
Project Brief
<http://www.worldbank.org/html/extdr/offrep/sas/ruralbrf/wtrsuply.htm>
The Software Technology Park Scheme
<http://www.soft.net>
The World Bank Group, Database of Information and Communication
Technologies Projects
< http://www.iicd.org/base/stories_overview>
The World Commission on Dams
<http://www.dams.org>
The Youth Employment Summit
<http://www.edc.org/spotlight/YES2001/role.htm>
The U.S. Library of Congress, "American Memory"
<http://memory.loc.gov/>
UNESCO, "Memory of the World"
<http://www.unesco.org/webworld/mdm/index_2.html>

Where Does Technology Fit in a Poverty Reduction Strategy?

Laurent Belsie, "Technologies That Changed the Way Humanity Lives."
Christian Science Monitor, 2000.
Carlos Braga, "Inclusion and Exclusion." Available at
<http://www.unesco.org/courier/1998_12/uk/dossier/txt21.htm>
Gro Harlem Brundtland, "Why Investing in Global Health is Good Politics."
Prepared remarks to the Council of Foreign Relations, New York, 6
December 1999.
Frances Cairncross, *The Death of Distance: How the Communications Revolution
Will Change Our Lives.* Cambridge, MA: Harvard Business School.
1997.
William J. Carrington and Enrica Detragiache, "How Big is the Brain
Drain?" Working Paper 98/102. Washington, D.C.: International
Monetary Fund. 1998.
Aly Coulibaly, "Africa is Out of the Technological Circle." *Panafrican News
Agency*, 3 November 1999.

Francis M Deng, "The Cow and the Thing Called "What": Dinka Cultural Perspectives on Wealth and Poverty." *Journal of International Affairs*, vol. 52, no. 1, Fall 1998.

Catherine Elton, "Peru's Potatoes Saved by Science." *Christian Science Monitor.* 15 March 2000.

Reed E. Hundt, "The Worldwide Communications Revolution: The Export of the American Idea," in Taylor Boas, *Rapporteur's Report,* Global Policy Program, Carnegie Endowment for International Peace, January 25, 2001.

Eric Hyman, "Production of Edible Oil for the Masses and By the Masses: The Impact of the Ram Press in Tanzania." *World Development* 21: 429-443. 1993.

Eric Hyman, "Technology and the Organisation of Production, Processing, and Marketing of Non-timber Forest Products." in *Current Issues in Non-timber Forest Products Research,* ed. by M.Ruiz-Perez and J.E.M. Arnold. Bogor, Indonesia: Center for International Forestry Research. 1996.

Eric Hyman, Jas Singh, and Edward Lawrence. "Building the Capacity of the Private Sector to Commercialize Technologies for Small-Scale Irrigation." *Science, Technology, and Development* 15 no. 1 (April): 63-91.1997.

A. Izaguirre, "Private Participation in Telecommunications—Recent Trends." Public Policy for the Private Sector Note No. 204. Washington, D.C.: World Bank. 1999.

Andy Jeans, Eric Hyman, and Mike O'Donnell. "Technology: The Key to Increasing the Productivity of Micro-Enterprises." *Small Enterprise Development* 2: 14-23. 1991.

Bill Joy, "Technology and Poverty in the 21st Century." *The International Poverty Gap: Investing in People and Technology to Build Sustainable Pathways Out.* (Washington, D.C.: The Aspen Institute. 2000.) Available at
<http://www.aspeninst.org/ipsp>

Peter T. Knight, "Lessons from infoDev Education Projects." Washington, D.C.: Knight-Moore Telematics for Education and Development/CDI. 2000. Available at
<http://www.knight-moore.com/pubs/Lessons_from_infoDev_Projects.html>

David Landes, *The Wealth and Poverty of Nations: Why Some Are so Rich and Some So Poor.* New York: W.W. Norton. 1999.

Judith Matloff, "Bargain Beets, Babushkas, and Russia's Internet." *Christian Science Monitor,* 3 February 2000.

Iqbal Quadir, "Loud and Near" *Alleviating Global Poverty: Technology for Economic and Social Uplift.* (Washington, D.C.: The Aspen Institute. 2001) Available at:
<http://www.aspeninst.org/ipsp>

Robert I. Rotberg, "Africa's Mess, Mugabe's Mayhem." *Foreign Affairs* 79:5. September/October 2000.

Andrew Shapiro, "Think Again." *Foreign Policy,* Winter 1998-1999.

Vandana Shiva, "Bioethics: A Third World Issue." Available at
<http://www.ratical.org/co-globalize/bioethics.html>.

Scott J. Wallsten, *An Empirical Analysis of Competition, Privatization and Regulation in Africa and Latin America.* Mimeo, Stanford Institute for Economic Policy Research. 1999.

James D. Wolfensohn, "Rethinking Development – Challenges and Opportunities." Remarks at the Tenth Ministerial Meeting of UNCTAD. Bangkok, Thailand, 16 February 2000. Available at <http://www.worldbank.org/html/extdr/extme/ jdwsp021600.htm>.

"Free to be Poor." *Economist,* 11 September 1999.

"Food: 'Feed the World' Used to Justify the New Technology." *Financial Times,* 6 December 1999.

"Latin America: Tropical Nets." *Financial Times,* 3 February 2000.

Technology to Empower the Poor to Improve Their Lives

Helena L. Chum and Ralph P. Overend, "Poverty Alleviation and Renewable Energy in a Sustainable Context." *Alleviating Global Poverty: Technology for Economic and Social Uplift.* (Washington, D.C.: The Aspen Institute. 2001) Available at: <http://www.aspeninst.org/ipsp>

Peter Huber, "Oil, Money and Pollution." *Forbes,* 15 May 2000.

Hyman, Eric. "An Economic Analysis of Small-Scale Technologies for Palm Oil Extraction in Central and West Africa." *World Development* 18, No. 3 (March): 455-476. 1990.

Marc Kaufman, "Biotech Crops Appear Safe, Panel Says." *Washington Post.* 6 April 2000.

Marc Kaufman, "Report Says Biotech Fails to Help Neediest Farmers." *Washington Post,* 11 July 2000.

Alexander F. McCalla and Lynn R. Brown, "Feeding the Developing World in the Next Millennium: A Question of Science?" *Agricultural Biotechnology and the Poor.* Washington, D.C.: National Academy of Sciences. 2000. Available at <http://www.cgiar.org/biotech/rep0100/Mccalla.pdf>.

National Renewable Energy Laboratory, "Energy Efficiency and Renewable Energy Technology Development in China – Protocol." Available at <http://www.nrel.gov/international/china/default.htm>.

Robert Paarlberg, "The Global Food Fight." *Foreign Affairs,* vol. 79, no. 3, pp. 34-38, May/June 2000.

Per Pinstrup-Andersen, Rajul Pandya-Lorch, and Mark Rosengrant, "The World Food Situation: Recent Developments, Emerging Issues, and Long-Term Prospects." *Food Policy Report.* Washington, D.C.: International Food Policy Research Institute. 1997.

Francisco Rodríguez and Ernest J. Wilson, III. "Are Poor Countries Losing the Information Revolution?" infoDev Working Paper. Washington, D.C.: World Bank. 2000.

M.S. Swaminathan, "Genetic Engineering and Food Security: Ecological and Livelihood Issues." *Agricultural Biotechnology and the Poor.* Washington, D.C.: National Academy of Sciences. 2000. Available at <http://www.cgiar.org/biotech/rep0100/swaminat.pdf>.

Ruth Walker, "Global Pact on GMOs Approved." *Christian Science Monitor,* 31 January 2000.

Qifa Zhang, "China: Agricultural Biotechnology Opportunities to Meet the Challenges of Food Production." *Agricultural Biotechnology and the Poor.*

Washington, D.C.: National Academy of Sciences. 2000. Available at <http://www.cgiar.org/biotech/rep0100/Zhang.pdf>.

World Bank Group, "Bank Supports Renewable Household Energy in Chad." Press Release. 2 June 1998. Available at <http://www.worldbank.org/html/extdr/extme/1790.htm>

"How Green Is Your Hydrogen?" *Economist*, 1 April 2000.

"A Soluble Problem." *Economist*, 25 March 2000.

"Aid for Aids." *Economist*, 29 April 2000.

"eXchange meets Dr. Mitra." *infoDev eXchange*, April-June 2000. Available at <http://www.infodev.org/news/exchange/exch200.pdf>

"Selling Fuel Cells." *Economist*, 1 July 2000.

"The Dawn of Micropower." *Economist*, 5 August 2000.

Technology, Poor People, and Job Creation

Carlos Braga, "The Networking Revolution: Opportunities and Challenges for Developing Countries." infoDev Working Paper. The World Bank Group. June 2000.

John Burgess, "A World Bank Marketplace of Ideas." *Washington Post*, 15 February 2000.

Thomas L. Friedman, "Social Safety Net." *New York Times*, 3 November 1999.

Eric Hyman, "Combining Credit and Technical Assistance: Alpaca Fiber Production and Processing in Bolivia." *Small Enterprise Development*,8, no. 3 (September): 42-50. 1997.

Eric Hyman, Jas Singh, and Edward Lawrence, "The Commercialization of Efficient Household Charcoal Stoves in Senegal." *Science, Technology, and Development*, 14, no.1: 1-20. 1996.

Charles S. Lee, "Hello World." *Far Eastern Economic Review*, 10 February 2000.

Pamela Mendels, "Program Trains Teachers in Cross-Border Sharing of Knowledge." *New York Times*, 15 March 2000.

Robert Reich, "Help the World Connect." *The Wall Street Journal*, 4 October 1999.

Jennifer L. Schenker, "A Wider Net." *Time Magazine*, 11 October 1999.

Lisa Stosch and Eric Hyman. "The El Salvador Coffee Production and Processing Project of EnterpriseWorks Worldwide." in *Business Development Services for Small and Microenterprises*, edited by Sunita Kapila. Ottawa: International Development Research Centre. Forthcoming.

The Task Force on Higher Education and Society, *Higher Education in Developing Countries: Peril and Promise*. Washington D.C.: World Bank Group. 2000.

"Tachyon and mPower3 Team to Create High-Performance Global Agricultural Extranet." Press Release. Tachyon Inc., 6 March 2000.

"Tachyon Establishes Tachyon de Mexico Bringing Fast Internet Access to Mesoamerica Region." Press Release. Tachyon Inc., 29 March, 2000.

"Cyber Laws Will Be Passed by May 17: Mahajan." *Economic Times*, 4 April 2000. Available at <http://www.soft.net/press/cyberlaw>.

"The Wiring of India." *Economist*, 27 May 2000.

Devising a Strategy to Harness Technology in Poverty Alleviation

Emmanuel Ablo and Ritva Reinikka, "Do Budgets Really Matter? Policy Research Working Paper 1926. Washington, D.C.: World Bank. 1998.

Mark Malloch Brown, "The Challenge of Information and Communications Technology for Development." Address by Administrator of the United Nations Development Programme. Tokyo, Japan, 3 July 2000. Available at <http://www.undp.org/dpa/statements>

Nayan Chanda, "Gates and Ghandi." *Far Eastern Economic Review*, 24 August 2000.

Barbara Crossette, "Gates Foundation Donates $26 Million to Fight Tetanus Abroad." *New York Times*, 22 November 1999.

Lynne Duke, "Foundations Target African Education." *Washington Post*, 25 April 2000, A5.

Geoff Dyer, "Brazil Tackles Its Digital Divide." *Financial Times*, 18 August 2000

Bradford S. Gentry and Daniel C. Esty, "Private Capital Flows: New and Addition Resources for Sustainable Development." *Bridges to Sustainability: Business and Government Working Together for a Better Environment.* Yale School of Forestry and Environmental Studies Bulletin Series, No. 101, 1997.

Tore Godal and Jeffrey D. Sachs, "Much Can Be Done to Make a Healthier World." *International Herald Tribune*, 28 January 2000.

Allen Hammond, "A Vision: How Emerging Technologies and Novel Partnerships-Especially Between the Private Sector and Civil Society-Could Accelerate Global Development, Especially in Poor Communities." *The International Poverty Gap: Investing in People and Technology to Build Sustainable Pathways Out.* (Washington, D.C.: The Aspen Institute. 2000.) Available at <http://www.aspeninst.org/ipsp>

Eric Hyman. "Making Foreign Aid More Relevant and Effective Through a Small-Scale Producers Strategy." *Journal of Environment and Development* 2, no. 2 (Summer): 79-95. 1993.

A. Izaguirre, "Private Participation in Telecommunications—Recent Trends." *Public Policy for the Private Sector Note No. 204.* Washington, D.C.: World Bank. 1999.

Joseph S. Nye, Jr., "Look Again, Globalization Isn't Bad for the Poor." *International Herald Tribune*, 13 April 2000.

Robert Paarlberg, "The Global Food Fight." *Foreign Affairs*, vol. 79, no. 3. May/June 2000, pp. 37-38.

Wolfgang H. Reinicke and Francis Deng with Jan Martin Witte, Thorsten Benner, Beth Whitaker, and John Gershman. *Critical Choices: The United Nations, Networks, and the Future of Global Governance.* Ottawa: International Development Research Centre. 2000.

Robert Schware, et al., *Internet Economic Toolkit for African Policy Makers.* Washington, D.C.: World Bank. 1999. Available at <http://www.infodev.org/projects/finafcon.htm>

Amartya Sen, *Development As Freedom.* New York: Anchor Books. 2000.

James D. Wolfensohn, "Let's Hear Everyone and Get On With Imaginative Solutions," *International Herald Tribune*, 28 January 2000.

James D. Wolfensohn, "Making Globalization Work for the Poor," presented at The Aspen Institute 50th Anniversary Symposium, August 19, 2000. Available at <http://www.aspeninst.org/fifty/wolfensohn.html>

African Development Bank, African Economic Research Consortium, Global Coalition for Africa, United Nations Economic Commission for Africa, and World Bank, *Can Africa Claim the 21st Century?* Washington, D.C.: World Bank. 2000.

The World Bank Group, "Business Partners for Development (BPD): International Partnerships Between Businesses, Governments, and Civil Society." Press Release (No. 99/1962/S). 3 October 1998.

"The World's Poor." *Harvard Magazine*, November-December 2000.

"Extending the Net." Monitor's View. *Christian Science Monitor*, 25 February 2000.

THE ASPEN INSTITUTE

INTERNATIONAL PEACE, SECURITY & PROSPERITY PROGRAM

The Aspen Institute International Peace, Security & Prosperity Program (IPSP) conducts high-level international leadership conferences to suggest strategies and actions through which greater peace, equity, prosperity, and sustainable development can be achieved in the early 21st century. Topics have included the new dimensions of national security, the role of intervention in managing conflict, conflict prevention, international poverty, and promoting peace in the Balkans. The current conference series is on global poverty.

IPSP conferences bring together changing sets of 20-30 international policy-makers and experts for in-depth roundtable dialogues. Participants are outstanding, diverse, and influential leaders from all global regions, including many from the developing world and an increasing number of next-generation leaders. Leading experts are commissioned to write papers that search out new ground on key topics. Conference speakers have included Jimmy Carter, José María Figueres, Nelson Mandela, Margaret Thatcher, Moeen Qureshi, George Soros, James Baker, William Perry, and Richard Goldstone. The program publishes a volume of conference conclusions and recommendations, papers, and speeches from each conference. These resource books are widely distributed to policymakers and others, are available on the Internet, and have been used in a number of university courses.

Director: Nancy Bearg Dyke
website: www.aspeninstitute.org/ipsp

Other Publications of the Aspen Institute International, Peace, Security & Prosperity Program

The International Poverty Gap: Investing in People and Technology to Build Sustainable Pathways Out
Report of the fall 1999 Aspen Institute conference assessing practical ways to close the gap between rich and poor nations and people and suggesting action agendas to implement the conclusions. The conference participants arrived at solid, timely recommendations for programs by which developed countries, universities, international institutions, corporations, and NGOs can more effectively work with developing countries in building sustainable pathways out of poverty.

Persistent Poverty in Developing Countries: Determining the Causes and Closing the Gaps
Report of the winter 1997 Aspen Institute conference of a diverse group of participants from around the globe who discussed the major causes of absolute poverty and feasible strategies, including a proposed "Market Plus" strategy, to combat existing poverty and its future spread.

Conflict Prevention: Strategies to Sustain Peace in the Post-Cold War World
Report of the summer 1996 Aspen Institute conference on conflict prevention that brought together 27 leaders and experts from 22 countries for dialogue on how violent conflict can be prevented now and into the 21st century.

Managing Conflict in the Post-Cold War World: The Role of Intervention
Report of the summer 1995 Aspen Institute conference of international leaders and experts who met over four days to discuss the sources of future conflict, lessons of the past, and whether and how the international community should intervene by political, economical, and military means in potential or ongoing conflicts.

International Peace and Security in a New World System
Report of the 1993 conference, which concentrated on how the end of the Cold War changed the dimension and definition of international security, including economics and new issues linked to sustainability, population growth, environmental degradation, and humanitarian crises, as well as traditional political and military concerns.

For further information on the publications and conferences of the
International Peace, Security, & Prosperity Program,
see http://www.aspeninstitute.org/ipsp/